T0121657

THE PREMIERSHIP MATCH DAY EXPERIENCE

'Through the Eyes of a Tiger'

Paul Collingwood

Order this book online at www.trafford.com
or email orders@trafford.com

Most Trafford titles are also available at major online book retailers.

© Copyright 2009 Paul Collingwood.
All rights reserved. No part of this publication may be reproduced, stored in a retrieval system, or
transmitted, in any form or by any means, electronic, mechanical, photocopying, recording, or
otherwise, without the written prior permission of the author.

Printed in Victoria, BC, Canada.

ISBN: 978-1-4269-1700-4

*Our mission is to efficiently provide the world's finest, most comprehensive book publishing
service, enabling every author to experience success. To find out how to publish your book, your
way, and have it available worldwide, visit us online at www.trafford.com*

Trafford rev. 11/4/2009

 www.trafford.com

North America & international
toll-free: 1 888 232 4444 (USA & Canada)
phone: 250 383 6864 ♦ fax: 812 355 4082

Also available by the same author:

AWAY WITH THE TIGERS

www.trafford.com

For Patsy, Elizabeth, Emma and Stephen

Contents

Introduction

24th April 1910

The black and amber class of 1910 travelled confidently to Oldham on the final day of the Football League season, requiring a mere point to secure top flight status. Victory would surely provide a springboard for future English and European domination, but they choked horribly and submitted to a tame 3-0 defeat. Thus, the tone had been set for the following century. We had missed out on promotion thanks to an inferior goal average, when a win would have seen us go up as champions.

Of course, there would have been no significant panic at the time. These were, quite literally, early days. Hull City Football Club was still in its infancy and even the most ardent of supporters would have to admit that promotion at this stage, after barely six years of existence, would have represented a major over achievement.

Indeed, your average Edwardian Tiger would have been in a philosophical mood as he supped his post match ale and wiped the froth from his ridiculously ample moustache.

'We were not ready for the dizzy heights of Division One anyway,' he would think. 'Far better that we spend another year in Division Two and then take it by storm in 1911,' he might have added. 'Hull is a large city with a huge fan base and it is surely just a matter of time before we claim our rightful place at the top table. Yes, it's just a matter of time.'

Twat! If only he had realised just how much time.

24ᵗʰ May 2008 (98 years and one month later)

The fourth official holds up his electronic board to reveal a bright green number four. We are four minutes from the Premiership. The Tigers lead Bristol City 1-0 at Wembley in the Championship Play-Off Final. This is going to be torture: four massive minutes.

I'm an optimistic person by nature, but not where Hull City are concerned. Their past is littered with near misses and if we blow this one, it will be the nearest miss of them all, topping even the miss of 1910.

Since that fateful season, there has been very little to shout about, certainly not in a positive sense, yet many success-starved natives of the city still suffer from the misapprehension that we once experienced some glory days. I'm sick of hearing about the glory days. We haven't had any glory days. The older generation continues to dwell on the so-called golden era of Raich Carter. Golden era, my arse! It wasn't even a silver era, unless we base it on the colour of his hair, which let's face it, was actually grey.

Carter's team of the forties fared no better than Horton's team of the eighties. In fact, if we're splitting hairs, Horton was statistically more successful, finishing sixth in the second division compared to Carter's seventh.

Because these people are so rooted in the gloomy past, they are unable to visualise a bright future. There is a reluctance to accept that Hull City could possibly survive in the Premiership. I do not subscribe to this pathetic theory of cowardice that we are not ready for promotion. History reminds us that it could be another 98 years before the chance presents itself again, and none of us will be around to enjoy it.

As expected, the four minutes of stoppage time at Wembley last an eternity as Bristol City pump a succession of long balls to the awkward Adebola. Seconds are remaining when Boaz Myhill manages a clean take from Lee Trundle's far post cross, and the roar of relief can be heard back in Hull. I've never heard such an audible reaction to such a regulation catch.

The black and amber end of the stadium collectively sense that Myhill's intervention signals the dawn of Premiership football for the city of Hull, and all eyes now lock on to the referee, awaiting that magical moment when we can all go just a little bit mental.

He raises the whistle to his lips, and blows hard. No one can hear it but we all know that the long wait is over. We are in the Premiership!

Instinctively, I form a triangular huddle with my two brothers, and we bounce up and down, screaming into each other's ears, but momentous occasions deserve profound quotes. Neil Armstrong was well primed for his moon landing in 1969, but I haven't 'dared to dream' yet, and I am totally unprepared for the moment. All I can think of is: 'We've f***ing done it!!'

Our emotions are embodied by Dean Windass as he comes rampaging off the bench, arms aloft, making a beeline for three tiers of delirious fans. Suddenly, the magnitude of his achievement hits him, and he curls up like a hedgehog to shed some tears. He's not the only one.

Now, finally, I can allow myself to dream about all the wonderful stadia that I can visit next season, although there may be some competition for tickets. I think another 40,000 City fans have just jumped on the bandwagon.

The Plan

Within days, the media have tried hard to dampen our euphoria by predicting that we will 'do a Derby.' In fact, it's not so much a prediction; it's more a promise. As we all know, Mark Lawrenson really knows what he's talking about, so I have devised an alternative form of entertainment for my twenty-stadium tour, just to give the season some purpose. As a little aside to the football, I will be conducting a survey to ascertain the greatest matchday experience. This sounds really boring, but bear with me.

It will not be a definitive guide, and I will not be seeking the views of the matchday masses through the use of exhaustive opinion polls. This will be my own private analysis, made on twenty particular days in history, so; if it's freezing cold, bucketing down with rain, my car breaks down and City get stuffed, the rating won't be too high.

Five main areas will be assessed on the day:

1. Accessibility – Nobody enjoys driving around in ever increasing circles in an unfamiliar town, so clear signposting and abundant parking is favourable. Neither do we enjoy getting marooned after the game, especially after a defeat, so a quick get away is also vital.

2. Facilities – Food and drink play a major role in a perfect matchday. A good ratio of pubs to fans is essential, and it helps

if they are within staggering distance of the ground. Food outlets must also be plentiful, and I don't like queues!

3. The Stadium – First impressions count for a lot here, inside and outside. Is it state of the art, or falling apart?

4. The Match – Any incidents of note during the ninety minutes of playing time will be taken into consideration: songs, fights, injuries, sending offs, pitch invasions, alien invasions – anything counts. A few goals would be nice too.

5. Character – This category provides an opportunity for some of the older crumbling grounds to gain some points, mentioning no names, as I don't want to alienate Portsmouth fans. Any number of factors may be included here: tradition, nostalgia, distinctive design features, and even the people. It's the fans that can give a club its soul.

By giving a mark out of ten for each area, I can judge every Premiership Matchday Experience with a score out of fifty. It may well be a close competition.

I can hardly wait for the fun to begin. I may only be in my forties, but it still feels like I've been waiting 104 years for this season to arrive.

EWOOD PARK

Saturday 23rd August 2008 – 3pm

Blackburn Rovers 1-1 Hull City

Paul Collingwood

Accessibility – 8 out of 10

Imagine driving into Hull along the A63 and seeing signs for major football grounds at Gilberdyke, Hessle, Ferriby, and Anlaby. Well, it's a bit like this on a short stretch of the M65 across the top of Lancashire. Junction 2 takes you up to Preston, junction 3 down to Bolton, junction 4 to Blackburn, and just another seven miles to the east, you arrive at Burnley. A couple of stops back down the M6 and it's Wigan, flanked on either side by Liverpool and Manchester.

Despite this abnormal cluster of clubs, Ewood Park is still very easy to locate. No sooner have I left junction 4, than I am guided through the gates of Darwen Vale Secondary School, where I can park for the surprisingly reasonable fee of £3. (Nice little earner for the school governors).

As I fumble for the correct change, some familiar faces stroll across the front of the school lawns, totally ignoring the 'Keep off the Grass' signs. It's my cousin Hugh, his wife Michele, and their two sons, Martin and Joseph. (Hereafter, they shall be referred to as the McAllisters). You may be hearing a lot about this family in the following pages as they have all managed to secure a place on the Away Direct scheme, unlike me, despite a grovelling letter to the club. The boys are now in their early twenties so were born into an era when our football club was an embarrassment to mankind. Their formative years were scarred by two relegations and an annual battle for survival, so full credit to their parents for keeping them within the Tigers fold. Boy, are they reaping the rewards now?

The stadium is still a fifteen-minute walk away but this poses no problem. We'll just jump onto the crest of a wave that Hull City have been riding for the last few years and float along with the hordes of black and amber clad fans, all eager to revel in the first away day of the Premiership season. Bring it on!

Facilities – 7 out of 10

Points are scored immediately for facilities as we stumble straight out of the car park into the arms of a welcoming pub. The *Golden Cup* is certainly convenient, but with most of today's four thousand strong

Tiger following appearing to be ahead of us in the queue for the bar, it may not be very productive. Actually, that last statement is not strictly true. Bars don't have queues. As usual, a massive crush of bodies are struggling desperately to catch the barmaid's eye, and the general rule in operation is, 'survival of the pushiest.' It's about time the post office system was adopted in pubs, where a polite recorded voice invites the next customer to step forward. Yes, I can just imagine it. 'Barmaid number 3 please.'

Young Joe dives into the throng and returns ten minutes later with five pints of the local brew – the pushy bugger. Finally, we are able to toast Hull City's first away game in the world's best league, against one of its founding members. The beer tastes good.

Several more drinking establishments are observed along the fifteen-minute hike to the ground, but very few Blackburn shirts are in evidence. Clearly, the locals avoid this direct route off the motorway, accepting that it will be infested with visitors on a match day.

Our supporters have been placed in the lower tier of the Darwen End Stand. This was built in 1990 and there is plenty of space inside for fans to mingle pre-match as they sup beer and risk a range of hot dogs and pies. Before taking my seat, I decide to check out the toilets, purely for research purposes. I'm greeted by a thick fog of smoke, created by all the naughty smokers that have been banned from practising their habit in public places. They are obviously operating under the hypothesis that toilet cubicles are not classified as public; in fact, you'd be hard pushed to find a more private place.

I am lured away from the toilets and into the fresh air of the Ewood Park arena by great booming echoes, which are emanating from the big screen in the corner. It is projecting highlights from Blackburn's opening day win at Everton and the volume appears to be stuck on the highest possible setting. If they are trying to psyche us out, it's not working. Down on the pitch, City's players seem unconcerned as they are put through their paces in the pre-match warm up.

The Stadium – 6 out of 10

Our approach to the ground brings us initially to the southwest corner, so my first impression is based on the striking Jack Walker Stand. You'll find a lot of things here named after the late Jack Walker. The opposite stand is similarly eponymous, bearing the name of Walker's Steel. A commemorative statue is now sited outside the ground and you can drive down Jack Walker Way, if the fancy takes you. His influence is inescapable, but any thoughts the club may have had about lending his name to the whole stadium were scuppered in 2002 when Leicester City named their new home after a certain brand of crisps.

A small building site that sits in front of the Darwen End spoils the external view. Within this ring-fenced area, it appears that a church may have been demolished, a sign of how priorities have changed in the last hundred years, as pilgrims now head to football grounds and shopping malls on Sundays. I pause to lament this changing trend before dashing off through the turnstiles to worship my false idols.

The view from Row 11 in the lower tier of the Darwen End is quite impressive. Three sides of the pitch are overlooked by large two-tiered structures, and in comparison to these, the inferior 30-year-old Walker's Steel Stand looks like it's in serious need of a makeover. If they could replace this with something that mirrors the Jack Walker Stand, then they'd really have a stadium. Trouble is, they'd never fill it.

The Match – 5 out of 10

Let's start by acknowledging Blackburn's part in creating a scintillating atmosphere within the stadium. This is not down to any singing by their fans, because there isn't any, but rather because they have allowed Tigers fans to pay on the day, which sees our loyal travelling supporters pack into the upper tier as well as the lower tier. Plenty of empty pockets of seats are visible on the other three sides and I'm sure Paul Ince is a little disappointed to see so many spaces as he is introduced to the crowd for his first home game in charge. At least this brings them to life a little and they manage to muster an encouraging cheer.

The opening exchanges are quite frenetic as both sides try to gain the initiative. This buzz of activity and the excitement of playing at a Premiership ground must have been a little overwhelming for City's players, for after four minutes there is an injury stoppage and they all rush to the touchline to rehydrate. It's not even a hot day. It never is in Blackburn.

Despite settling well, and looking quite comfortable at this level, we controversially fall behind after 38 minutes as Jason Roberts springs our offside trap and slots home. Of course, we are all convinced that it is at least three yards offside and the big screen seems to confirm our view so everyone has a right go at the linesman (I still refuse to call them referee's assistants).

My brother, Mike, in Madrid, requested text alerts from me but I'm a notoriously slow texter and in the middle of trying to describe the legality of Robert's strike, I look up to see Richard Garcia's header looping over Paul Robinson for the equaliser. After a brief unhinged celebration I scrub the text and begin to compose a new, more positive one, but even as I do this, the City defence come under pressure and I fear that I'll soon be deleting this one as well.

So far, the City contingent has been almost unrelenting in its vocal support with little reply from the rest of the arena. Naturally, there was an excitable response when Blackburn scored, but that only lasted for 90 seconds, as they only sing when they're winning.

The second half is reasonably entertaining, but chances are at a premium. Santa Cruz shows a glimpse of his quality with their two best chances, and there is a worrying cameo from our new French signing, Bernard Mendy, who seems so keen to impress that he mis-times all his challenges including one spectacular diving header, where he completely misses the ball.

Mendy apart, we defend competently and reach stoppage time without too many alarms. Four minutes are added, and we have two great chances to win it. A blistering volley from Caleb Folan flies straight into Robinson's chest and then Ricketts advances into the area before firing weakly at the Beverley man.

All in all, a good point, but we could have sneaked it in the closing seconds. The point puts us third in the Premiership. Yes, I know we've only played two games, but it still looks bloody good.

Character – 6 out of 10

Blackburn gain points for character just for being founder members of the league, and also for being the longest tenants of any Football League ground – 118 years, to be precise. The place is steeped in history, and a little piece of this has been preserved outside. Whereas the church was deemed 'surplus to requirements,' an immaculate row of cottages nearby has been served a stay of execution, and on closer inspection, I learn why.

A wall-mounted plaque by the front door of the central dwelling explains that this is the birthplace of Harry Healless. (No, I haven't heard of him either). Apparently he was captain of Blackburn's 1928 FA Cup wining side, which memorably beat Huddersfield 3-1. (No, I don't remember that one either) but it is clearly important to the people of Blackburn. Further research tells me that Harry made several appearances for England and lived until 1972. It doesn't say whether he died in the cottage too.

Ewood Park itself is low on character, except for the older East Stand which does still evoke that slight nostalgic feeling. Two large floodlight pylons are required on this side and it dawns on me that these no longer feature in designs of the new big stadia.

Summary

It's a nice starter to whet our appetites: an established Premiership side with bags of tradition and a redeveloped 31,000 seater stadium. We have gained a decent point too and remain unbeaten in the Premiership. Magic!

It's a flaming long drive back to Hertfordshire though.

Matchday Experience Total – 32 out of 50

ST JAMES' PARK

Saturday 13th September 2008 – 3pm

Newcastle United 1-2 Hull City

Accessibility – 5 out of 10

St James' Park is actually quite easy to find, but then again, I'm not driving. Martin has been granted the privilege on this occasion, so my only duty for the journey is to read all the back pages of the Saturday papers. Michele is the self-appointed navigator, leaving Hugh, Joe and me to accept the restricted leg space and bum space in the back.

High marks will not be scored for accessibility, though, as parking turns out to be a complete nightmare. Several circuits of unplanned sightseeing are forced upon us as we seek out a parking spot, but it is mildly amusing throughout this time, to observe Martin's gradual submission to road rage. Michele finally cracks and winds the window down to request directions from a steward, but he is not the sharpest tool in the box. He directs us to a small pay and display area, which would struggle to serve our local Tesco Express, let alone a 52,000 seater stadium. Our joyous tour continues, therefore, and the circuits spiral ever further from the ground. Joe's suggestion that our agitated driver might want to drop us at the gates of St. James' and catch up with us later is quickly rebuffed, and not very politely either.

Tension is building, the petrol gauge is dropping and drinking time is ebbing away, when finally, a space is spotted and Martin reverses into a tight spot on the corner of a back street. With great relief, I leap from the car to stretch my legs and air some seriously sweaty armpits.

The walk towards the stadium is fairly straightforward and quiet, until a trio of Geordie youngsters pedal furiously by on their bikes (or possibly someone else's bikes: hence, the great haste). At this point, Martin thinks it will be really funny to ask the little lads, where the ground is, even though the massive Milburn Stand is blocking out all the sunlight straight ahead of us. The three bikers apply the breaks and display a good judge of character by looking at him as if he's a complete idiot. The gang leader steps forward, points at the ground and delivers a reply in a strong Byker Grove accent.

'It's right over there dopey! Ya must be blind man.'

Martin offers his sincere thanks and then shuts up. He knows when he's met his match. He's just been well and truly put in his place by a streetwise little ten year old. Well, at least we've found the ground.

Facilities – 8 out of 10

The hunt for beer and food begins, but we are soon distracted by all the protests outside the stadium. King Kevin Keegan has walked out on the club, blaming the interference of Mike Ashley and Dennis Wise in transfer matters. Roughly translated, this means that they are not giving Kevin handfuls of cash, preferring instead to secretly sign young players from abroad; players that Kevin has never even heard of. Keegan enjoys God-like status on Tyneside, so the fans are one hundred percent behind him. Their thoughts are summed up on a huge banner, which has been unfurled in front of the Gallowgate End, outside the *Shearer Bar*.

It reads: 'WANTED – For crimes against Newcastle United – Mike 'Fattyboy' Ashley & Dennis 'Ratface' Wise – Last seen being clueless and interfering in the vicinity of St James' – REWARD OFFERED.

The banner is attracting a fair amount of media attention, with presenters and cameramen from all of the major TV channels swarming around interviewing a succession of disgruntled locals. Strangely, as part of the demonstrations, home fans are also planning to boycott food outlets within the ground, believing that this is going to have some kind of indirect influence on Ashley's tenure. This policy obviously also includes the purchase of match programmes, as we are given a bit of abuse when we approach the stand nearby. The lonely looking vendor is clearly getting wound up and he tells them all in no uncertain terms to 'go forth and multiply.'

It seems that all of today's shenanigans may well work in our favour; not from a football point of view, but from a pub grub point of view. We slip almost unnoticed into the spacious 'state of the art' Shearer Bar, and find it half empty. The customary scrum at the bar does not exist, and within seconds, we are knocking back Newcastle Brown Ale whilst watching the early Premiership clash between Liverpool and Manchester United.

Not all of the home fans have gone along with the boycott – a Geordie and his pint are not easily parted – and our black and amber attire acts like a magnet to them. One larger than life lady in the garish purple Newcastle away shirt sidles over to wish us the best of luck. Her sentiments are genuine, as she believes that a Newcastle defeat will hasten the end of the present regime.

'Let's hope your defence are in such a generous mood,' I declare.

'Defence? Defence? This is Newcastle man! We don't have a defence. Where the hell have you been for the last fifteen years?'

We are interrupted by another depressed local with a dark cloud hanging over his head. He is selling dodgy looking tickets for a half time draw, and even though it looks like a sure-fire scam, we part with our pounds, before pressing him for some Toon team news. Instead of giving us the starting line up, he reels off a list of injured players who will *not* be appearing, particularly strikers, which makes us think that we might actually get some points from this match. Then we mention Alan Smith, and his cloud darkens.

'Don't get me going on Alan Smith,' he groans.

But it's too late. He has already got going. He launches into a statistical analysis of Smith's strike rate. Apparently, he only scored one goal in over forty appearances last season, and that was in a friendly. 'Call him a striker?' he concludes. 'He couldn't strike a fucking match!'

Eventually, we move upstairs, where another queue-free bar is available to keep us fed and watered. This really is a first class facility and Mr. Shearer must be rightly proud to have such an establishment named after him. We are assured by the punters that it is normally heaving on match days, so the timing of this fixture couldn't have been better from a thirsty City fan's perspective. The glass fronted building looks out onto the stay-away protesters below, who are now laying their striped tops in the middle of the road, allowing cars to drive over them. I think they are losing the plot.

Our long stay here means that I don't get too much time to check out other facilities. The standard array of food outlets are available inside the ground but I don't make my usual assessment of the hot dogs, as I've already had one in the Shearer's, and very nice it was too.

The Stadium – 8 out of 10

It's big, but it looks a bit like a giant multi-story car park from the outside, and it feels like it once I'm inside, scaling hundreds of steps to reach the upper tier of the Sir John Hall Stand. But, the view from the top is worth the climb. St James' is a stadium of two halves, and we are in the huge half. I am in awe of the enormous Milburn Stand to my right and I smile a little smile of disbelief that Hull City are now visiting such majestic arenas on a fortnightly basis.

Looking to the front, I can see right over the top of the Gallowgate End, far into the distant hills. The view extends to the left, above and beyond the East Stand. This is the stand that you generally see on the television screens, where the words 'NEWCASTLE UNITED' are printed in bold black capital letters along the bright white front edge of the rooftop. My lofty vantage point must give me one of the best views in the city, although a cynical person might suggest that the best view of Newcastle can be found in the rear-view mirror of your car.

It's not until the game gets under way that I note the absence of a scoreboard and a clock, unless it is hidden away in the lower tier of our stand. Then, well into the second half, I spot a small digital device tucked between two advertising boards just near the corner flag, counting down the ninety minutes. Call me slow on the uptake, but it turns out that there are four of these, one in each corner, and they all have my surname sitting next to them in large letters in the form of adverts for *Collingwood Insurance.* You tend to miss these things when the football on offer is so absorbing, and it turns out to be a very entertaining match.

The Match – 8 out of 10

Despite all the local unrest and threatened boycotts, there don't appear to be many empty seats in the ground. The folk up here love their football too much and have rejected the tempting alternative of traipsing round the Metro Centre with the family. A banner held aloft by one elderly die-hard fan nearby attempts to point out that they're not here to line Mike Ashley's pockets. 'I'm only here to support my team,' it reads.

A highly vocal section of home fans are located just to our right, and several of the early choral offerings make it patently clear that they want Kevin Keegan back. They have unwittingly provided the Hull faithful with some early ammunition here as we harmoniously ask: 'Where's your Keegan gone?' to the tune of the 1971 classic from *Middle of the Road.*

Marlon King's successfully converted penalty after half an hour just encourages us even more, and we decide to let everyone know that we also possess a manager with God-like status, except ours is not prone to walking out.

'Browny, Browny, give us a wave…' we all bellow, followed by a rousing cheer when he gladly obliges. The same request is then made of Kevin Keegan, followed by a round of boos when he fails to respond (obviously, as he's probably on a beach in Spain).

We get to half-time with the lead still intact. I flick through the match programme in an attempt to pass the time and calm my nerves. The centre pages are filled with action shots from their last home fixture with Bolton, which the Magpies won 1-0. The key moments from the game are represented by photos of Shay Given's penalty save and Michael Owen's goal, from a fine glancing close range header. How ironic that the pivotal moments in today's first half have been almost identical, except that Given couldn't quite grasp King's penalty, and Myhill pulled off a great reflex save from Owen's close range glancing header. It's a fine line…

If we thought we were in heaven at half-time, then we reach it for sure within ten minutes of the restart when King breaks away to score his and City's second. It's a cool finish by the Wigan loanee, and it surely finishes off Newcastle. The singing is re-ignited, and gloriously, St. James' Park is filled with echoes of, 'You're being mauled by the Tigers.' As usual, our irritating mauling actions seriously wind up the opposing fans, and they strike back with a work of sheer genius:

'What the fucking hell was that…'

But there is no let up in the 'Geordie baiting,' and our next chant asks them if they might be Grimsby in disguise. Again, the opposition give great consideration to an appropriate response, and after a brief pause to pool their creative juices, they come up with another gem, 'Who the fucking hell are you…'

I don't think their hearts are really in this.

It can't be a very enjoyable experience, watching your side take a pasting from unfancied Hull City, but secretly, they must be pleased, as it will surely now bring about the downfall of 'Fatty Ashley' and 'Ratface

Wise.' It nearly gets worse for them soon afterwards, and better for us, when Turner heads home Dawson's corner at the far post, but the referee decides to throw Newcastle a lifeline by creating an infringement. Nothing illegal happened as the ball swung over, although Given did clatter into his own player. Maybe the ref confused the teams, as City's dark grey tops are hard to distinguish from Newcastle's black and white stripes, and even his demand that we borrow white shorts and socks from our hosts has failed to solve the problem. Why couldn't we have used our black and amber stripes? Do people still watch on black and white sets nowadays?

City being City, we are made to sweat for the last ten minutes when new Spanish signing, Xisco, pulls a goal back, but Newcastle's disheartened and rudderless side are unable to penetrate. With the final whistle, another landmark in Hull City's history is reached; our first away Premiership win.

Character – 7 out of 10

The people provide much of the character around St. James' Park. There is nothing more entertaining than a Geordie with something to complain about, and they've certainly got plenty to chew on this week. We seem to spend the day acting as temporary agony aunts while they pour out their troubles with a succession of hilarious one-liners. In this respect, they bear similarity to the natives of Liverpool, except the Geordies really are funny.

The stadium itself is quite distinctive, and as soon as you walk out of the stairwell and gaze out across the pitch, you know that you are in St. James' Park. Many of today's freshly built stadia are like peas from the same pod, so it is refreshing to see, that despite a fair degree of recent modernisation, St. James' is still a unique ground.

There's still half an hour to the kick off when I first take my place, so most of the seats are empty, and I am struck by another rarity. All of the seats are grey. Most clubs tend to opt for reds and blues so this is another feature that allows this stadium to stand alone. Then I realise where I've seen grey seats before – the KC Stadium.

Paul Collingwood

Summary

It has been a grand day out; the sort of day that we all dreamt about, but thought would never happen. We have climbed back up to fourth in the Premiership and have restored some pride after the 5-0 drubbing by Wigan.

It is a shame that the Sunday papers will probably focus on Newcastle's woes rather than City's achievements. I can't help thinking that these Geordie folk are getting this crisis thing a little out of proportion. They don't know what a crisis is. Ten years ago, Hull City were 92nd in the league, with Mark Hateley as a manager and David Lloyd as an owner. Now, that's what I call a crisis… man!

Matchday Experience Total – 36 out of 50

THE EMIRATES STADIUM

Saturday 27th September 2008 - 5.30pm

Arsenal 1-2 Hull City

Paul Collingwood

Accessibility – 7 out of 10

If you decide to arrive by tube, which any right-minded person would, then the Emirates Stadium is quite easy to find. My starting point is Hemel Hempstead, so initially I take a train to Euston, which bizarrely, is full of screaming babies. It's a relief when we stop at Watford Junction, and one of the balling babes leaves the carriage. In its place, we get a number of red-shirted glory-seeking Arsenal fans who really should be travelling up to Sheffield today to watch Championship football with their real team, Watford.

From Euston, it is just two stops on the tube to Highbury & Islington, although I could have changed and gone to Arsenal Station, which is a bit closer.

My companion for the day is my 9-year-old son, Stephen. He's coming as a neutral observer as he has no affinity for Hull City; in fact he has become very anti Hull City. I blame Stuart Elliott. Stephen's first game was three years ago at Burnley and Elliott should have had a hat-trick that night to secure my son's eternal loyalty with a storming win. Instead, we lost 1-0; he was uninspired, and he has now adopted Manchester United as his favourites, thanks mainly to the superstar status of Cristiano Ronaldo.

The stadium is just ten minutes from the tube station, if you believe the Arsenal website, but it turns out to be more like twenty. Clearly, you're supposed to run. I wouldn't want to drive into the area without pre-booked parking arrangements either, as it is very built up, the roads are busy and space is tight.

Of course, the walk back to the station after the game takes even longer. Arrival is staggered, but departure is simultaneous, and the vast majority of the 60,000 crowd are returning by tube. We find ourselves shuffling down a side street at a pace that would frustrate a snail, and even then we keep being halted as the police create a traffic light system at the t-junction ahead, only letting out a few at a time. We get there in the end, and it is plain sailing thereafter.

Facilities – 8 out of 10

There is no shortage of eating facilities en route to the ground, with a range of take-aways and small cafés, but I wouldn't fancy testing my immune system in any of them. It looks like there is plenty of work here to keep the Environmental Health Department occupied for years to come. I'm sure I see Matt Allwright from BBC's Rogue Restaurants sitting in the bay window of one establishment. Maybe he is just an Arsenal fan.

The pubs on this stretch have also seen better days, and they all appear to be at full capacity as scores of drinkers spill out onto the narrow pavements. It is a warm September day; with temperatures touching 70°C, and everyone seems happy to wear their short-sleeved replica tops. So far, I haven't seen any Hull City shirts outside the pubs, suggesting that we're navigating a bit of a no-go area for away supporters. It's just as well that I'm not in club colours today, having wangled a couple of free passes in the Arsenal end from a contact in the Holloway Police.

The inconvenient tea-time kick off induces rumbling stomachs, so we quicken our pace and head for the ground to check out the food outlets within, and it turns out to be a wise choice. A number of queue-free hatches reside beneath the upper tier of the Blue Quadrant and there is ample space for us to roam around and view the TV screens while Stephen consumes a hot dog as long as his arm. I'm not quite sure where he puts it, but he somehow polishes it off and proceeds to make short work of a box of mini doughnuts, which you can dunk into a small pot of raspberry jam. The layout here is very similar to Wembley with a number of breakfast-bar type surfaces available, where you can safely dunk your doughnuts to your heart's content, free from the fear of jam spillage.

Large clear glass windows offer an excellent view of the gathering crowds below, which is preferable to watching the constant re-runs of Arsenal's 6-0 mid-week thrashing of Sheffield United in the Carling Cup. It's a bit scary to think that none of this young side are yet good enough to make today's starting eleven. Gulp!

Paul Collingwood

The Stadium – 10 out of 10

'It's better than Wembley,' remarks Stephen, as the giant Emirates spaceship comes into view. Despite his tender years, he is already becoming a connoisseur of football grounds, this being his eighth. Bold red lettering on the stadium wall, accompanied by two large Gunners badges immediately inform you that this is the home of Arsenal Football Club, whereas at Wembley, there just seemed to be lots of glass. Take away the famous arch, and our national stadium could be mistaken for a shopping complex.

We mount a grand wide staircase and pause at the top to consult a map, which explains the four coloured quadrants. Hull City's section is in the lower tier of the red quadrant, just near the corner flag, but Stephen and I will be sitting high up above the opposite corner. The correct turnstile is found and we insert our borrowed passes into a bleepy mechanism, before advancing into enemy territory.

An option to take the lift to our seats is offered, but we by-pass the small queue and give each other a race up the stairs, which nearly does me in for the day. There is plenty of time to satisfy our hunger (see previous section) before checking out the famous padded seats. Upon taking our place, Stephen confirms his opinion that the Emirates is better than Wembley. Of course, all the seats here are padded, not just the expensive ones, and even Peter Crouch would be unable to complain about the leg room.

There is half an hour to kick off, and the stands are sparsely populated, but it is still a terrific view. I give myself the customary pinch on the arm. Good, it hurts, so I'm not dreaming. Hull City really are coming to grounds like this to play Premiership football.

I become distracted by the trail of honours from Arsenal's glittering past that are displayed along the upper balcony edge. For each success, there is a white silhouette of the relevant trophy on a red background, followed by the year of triumph. They boast enough of these to complete an entire circuit of the stadium. This is not an idea that we could mimic back at the KC.

The roof extends a long way out towards the pitch, which creates an indoor feel, and the mild weather aids this effect. The undulating nature of the back seats in the upper tier produces an almost parallel flow to the ceiling, which looks disturbingly warped as a result. I just hope it is meant to look like this. There are two points where the gap between seats and roof widens in order to accommodate the big screens. Yet again, we are treated to the six mid-week goals that sunk the hapless Blades.

With five minutes to go before kick off, an alarming number of Gooners have still failed to make it out of the bars and into their seats. It makes me suspicious that they may not be taking Hull City very seriously.

The Match – 10 out of 10

In a desperate attempt to whip up the crowd into something approaching a state of enthusiasm, the MC reels off the Arsenal teamsheet by playing a little party game that is extremely pantomime-like in its execution. As the photos, numbers and names are displayed on the big screens, he yells out the first name of each player, and the crowd is expected to respond in deafening tones with the surnames. The kids seem to be up for it, but the adults look a little embarrassed, or maybe their French, Spanish and African pronunciation is not up to scratch. I much prefer the less complicated version, where the whole name is read out, and we reply with a simple, 'hurray!'

It is the City fans that find their voice first, and they are clearly audible from the opposite side of the ground, even though they represent just 5% of the total crowd. Like myself, they can hardly believe that they are here, and they are determined to deliver their full repertoire of songs. This feeling of disbelief was explained well by my cousin's wife, Michele, when I bumped into her outside the ground. She had met some Arsenal fans at a service station on the edge of London and was explaining that it was more than 200 miles from Hull.

'So how long did it take you to get here?' asks the Gooner.

'104 years,' she replies.

To be fair to the Arsenal fans, they do generate a fair bit of noise once the game gets under way, and once they've vacated the bars. They respond well to the provocation of the City supporters and the wonky roof does a good job of keeping the sound inside the stadium. The atmosphere is good.

Phil Brown's bold 4-3-3 formation takes Arsenal by surprise and their fans are a little quieter by half-time when it is still 0-0: clearly, we have come here to play.

Despite the parity, a chap behind me remains upbeat. 'I can't see Hull scoring,' he confidently predicts. True, we haven't created too many clear-cut opportunities, but I still make a mental note of where he is sitting, just in case City score, and I get the chance to ram the comment down his throat, or maybe up his arse; I'll decide later.

Arsenal are suffering from their recurring affliction of trying to walk the ball into the net. Two or three very good opportunities have already been wasted in the first half when they made that extra unnecessary pass, so Paul McShane decides to help them out after 54 minutes by bundling the ball over his own goal line. It comes at the end of a mazy run from Theo Walcott, which induces panic in the Tigers defence, causing McShane to apply the fatal touch.

At this point, everyone in the stadium, and everyone watching around the world on Setanta, expect Hull City to cave in. Well, the world is in for a shock.

City's heroic defence holds firm during the ensuing onslaught, setting the stage for Geovanni, our ex-Barcelona, Brazilian international. There appears to be little danger when our new idol receives possession on the left touchline, but he cuts inside and unleashes an unstoppable 30-yard screamer right into the top corner. I forget where I am, and instinctively stand to applaud, but I don't need to worry about blowing my cover. Several Gooners around me have done the same thing, such was the wonder of the strike, and we all agree that we have just seen the Goal of the Season.

There is hardly time for the dust to settle before Daniel Cousin forces a corner with a low deflected shot. We are really taking the game to Arsenal now and I can sense the unease around me. Dawson's corner is whipped into the box, and incredibly, Cousin rises highest to plant a header into the top corner. This time I manage to suppress my natural instincts. Instead, I lean across Stephen and squeeze the life out of his arm. He lets out a little yelp.

Unable to dance around with delight, I derive pleasure from watching three thousand crazed City fans performing a great impression of the Muppet Show audience. I sincerely wish I was down there to share the moment, but it is a wonderful sight to behold.

The world still fully expects Arsenal to come back and win. They are in for another shock. A mixture of resolute defending and inspired goalkeeping from Myhill see us edge ever closer to the final whistle. Walcott is substituted: good sign. Vela, scorer of a mid-week hat-trick, comes on: bad sign.

I find myself thinking that a draw would still be a good result, but then Gallas' late header crashes against the bar before being scrambled to safety, and I realise that this is going to be our day. There is still time for another crucial save from Myhill before the referee sends us back to dreamland. We have been there a few times over the last year, but this victory is the most unexpected. It is only Arsenal's second ever defeat at the Emirates and their first for eighteen months.

Naturally, City's players spend a lengthy spell milking the applause from our ecstatic band of supporters, but they then receive another warm round of applause from the rest of the stadium, the ones who haven't already buggered off. Either, there are 20 000 Hull City infiltrators, or the Arsenal fans are actually gracious in defeat. It's the icing on the cake for the greatest victory in our history.

Character 6 out of 10

This is a brand new stadium, so let's face it; we are unlikely to come across too many traditional features to take me on a trip down memory lane, unless you count the glut of grotty pubs and restaurants in the surrounding area. My panorama from the blue quadrant bar also takes in several unsightly blocks of high-rise flats and a stretch of railway track, which only seems to accommodate lengthy plodding corroded freight trains. It amazes me that room was ever found amongst all of this to construct an enormous 21st century football stadium.

No, to gain 'character points,' these new arenas need to provide me with some distinctive aspects of design, which give them an identity, setting them apart from countless other new venues across the country. Inside the Emirates, it's the tall metal posts silhouetted against the skyline at the top of the stands that fulfil this criteria. Stephen recognises these from the highly realistic FIFA 08 game on his Play Station, where

Hull City have taken on Arsenal many times, although I don't ever remember the virtual Arsenal side allowing City to walk away with a 2-1 win.

Summary

Before the game, I had been a little in awe of all the Arsenal fans as they surrounded me on the train. I may even have felt ever so slightly jealous that they had the good fortune to support one of the best sides in Europe. I felt like a fish out of water – an impostor. Did Hull City really belong in this world?

But after the game, I feel quite sorry for them as they lick their fresh wounds. It can't be very pleasant, being mauled by the Tigers.

Matchday Experience Total – 41 out of 50

WHITEHART LANE

Sunday 5th October 2008 – 3pm

Tottenham Hotspur 0-1 Hull City

Accessibility – 7 out of 10

It is a foul Autumn day: dull, cold, wet and windy with horizontal driving rain, but as a dedicated Dad, I'm required to spend the early hours standing out in the middle of a field. Stephen's Under 10's football fixture has survived the heavy precipitation, so match day number 4 is put on hold. The game finally finishes at 10.45, and I immediately squelch off to the railway station for an emergency removal of saturated socks and trousers on the back seat of the car. Don't worry; I've brought a change of clothing.

The journey to Seven Sisters should be straight forward enough, but Sunday kick offs lay themselves at the mercy of motorway maintenance men and railway engineers, because of course, no one ever goes anywhere on a Sunday; it's a day of rest.

Sure enough, just as I've parked my damp buttocks into a seat on the Euston train, my brother Peter phones to warn me of a suspended service on the Piccadilly Line, so we can no longer rendezvous at Seven Sisters. He's got my match ticket, so we agree to divert to Manor House on the Victoria Line. This turns out to be a blessing in disguise, as a bus is waiting to whisk us straight to the ground, saving us from the monsoon rain. If we had walked from Seven Sisters, I would have needed a third pair of trousers.

With growing concern for the large amounts of water dropping from the leaden skies, we wait outside the Spurs Shop for our second rendezvous of the day. The McAllister family soon show, and we head into the store to begin our inspection of facilities, or maybe we just want to keep dry.

Facilities – 7 out of 10

The proprietors of the shop must love the rain. You can hardly move inside, so you need to browse with real conviction, or the security guys soon suss you out, and guide you back out into the rain. Ten minutes are killed searching for a rack of discount Berbatov, shirts, but they're probably all in a landfill site by now.

I go back out, and ready myself for rendezvous number three, with an old college friend, another Pete. He was a big fan of Spurs back in the eighties (Waddle and Hoddle etc.) but Hull City got into his blood in 1984 when I took him to see a run-of-the-mill Division 3 match at Orient. The Tigers famously came back from 4-1 down with 20 minutes left to win 5-4. He's taken a keen interest ever since.

Pete, and his son Joe keep us waiting, even though we spoke just fifteen minutes ago and he assured me that they were only five minutes away. How hard can it be to find the great big blindingly obvious Spurs Shop? It turns out that there are three Spurs Shops.

Just across the road sits a handy little pub – *The Corner Pin* – but it doesn't look too welcoming. The peculiar name is explained by a weather-beaten sign high up on the outer wall, swinging in the blustery breeze, depicting the corner flag on a football pitch. It is becoming more weather-beaten by the second, and so are we, so a member of the local constabulary is quizzed about its suitability for away fans. His reply lacks encouragement.

'Even the police don't go in there mate!'

It leaves us with no option. The only safe bet for finding instant food and drink is to enter the ground and queue for a hotdog. City's impressive start to the season means that tickets are increasingly hard to come by, so we will be sitting with the enemy for the second week running.

Our route to the West Stand turnstile takes us straight through the players' car park, and a more expensive and exotic collection of vehicles you couldn't wish to see, unless you stumbled into the NEC during the National Motor Show: Bentleys, Lamborghinis, Porsches… you name it, and several 4 x 4's, which presumably belong to the wives, to help them navigate the steep, treacherous, muddy roads of North London. No wonder this bunch of superstars are bottom of the league; they've got more money than sense.

We're soon in the queue for food in the upper tier reception area (am I making it sound like a posh hotel)? My taste buds are tempted by a mouth-watering heap of pasties in the rear display case, but my request for the traditional Cornish tucker generates a worried frown on the face of the vendor. His limited command of English seems to be preventing him from explaining the technical hitch.

' Err… no pasties…err…pasties not err…err…'

'Hot?' I suggest.

'Yes, hot. Pasties not hot.'

As an inadequate alternative, I am offered a hotdog, which presumably he couldn't offer anyone before, as he didn't know the word for hot.

These outlets stretch along the West Stand for as far as the eye can see and the queues are not too bad. If there's one thing I hate, it's queues, and food outlets at football grounds are usually accompanied by lengthy ones, so well done Spurs.

The Stadium – 7 out of 10

I've enjoyed better first impressions of grounds. The final stop on the 275 bus route does not provide the greatest viewpoint for Whitehart Lane, and the grey depressing weather is no help. Apparently, the eastern perspective is far more attractive, but I can't really be bothered to take a look.

The interior is more inspiring, and my seat in the upper tier of the West Stand provides the perfect vantage point. It is a tidy two-tiered ground, and the 38 000 bright royal blue seats are gradually filling up as we approach kick off time. Two large screens are built into the rooftops at either end and they provide us with all the pre-match team news. Unsurprisingly, City begin with the same line-up that shook the foundations at the Emirates, while Spurs give a start to Fraizer Campbell. Several choruses of the Fraizer Campbell song ring out from the City contingent, which is just six or seven seats to my right. We will never forget his contribution to our promotion. Of course, he should be a permanent Tiger by now, but double-crossing Fergie used him as a pawn in the Berbatov deal, so he found himself on loan at Spurs for the season, poor sod.

The Match – 7 out of 10

It's still sinking in that City can attract Brazilian internationals to the club, but Geovanni helps to hammer it home after nine minutes by curling in a sublime free kick, as only Brazilians can. On the back of last week's belter against Arsenal, he appears to be running his own Goal of the Season competition.

A couple of lads next to Peter leap into the air in an act of unrestrained celebration, and they're not the only ones. It seems that quite a number of infiltrators have joined us in the West Stand, but the stewards don't make a fuss. Nor do the disillusioned Londoners around me.

Meanwhile, three thousand fans to my right are in dreamland, and it's not long before their songs predict the sacking of Juande Ramos. Questions are then posed about whether they may be Arsenal in disguise.

An open game of attacking football ensues with Spurs hitting the woodwork twice, and City once, but we reach half time still a goal to the good.

We go far more defensive in the second half and only create one worthwhile opportunity when Marlon King is released for a one-on-one with Gomez, but the Brazilian wins the dual. A series of near misses, saves and blocks are required and Fraizer clearly remembers where his loyalties lie as he refuses to put the ball in the back of the net. I'm not sure what Darren Bent's excuse is though. We hold on to take all three points – that's six out of six in North London within a week. Incredibly, we have climbed to third in the Premiership, and with the international break next week, we'll have two whole glorious weeks to enjoy it.

Character – 6 out of 10

I'm still not entirely sure how to quantify the character of a stadium and its surrounding area, but if the definition is 'run down and grotty,' then the streets around Whitehart Lane come up trumps, although, to be fair, the damp weather does them no favours. However, I'm more on the look out for 'charming and traditional' so most of the points are gained by the inside of the stadium.

It has changed since my last visit in the late eighties and the impressive shelf has long gone, but I'm pleased to see that the distinctive cockerel still resides proudly on top of a golden football high up on the roof. It must be heavy, for this is the only roof in the ground which needs to be held up by large metal posts, so the spectators at the back of the stand can enjoy the traditional practice of leaning into someone else's lap whenever the action hides itself from view.

Summary

What a contrast to my last visit to watch Hull City here in 1981. Spurs were on the road to Wembley and we were on the road to nowhere, but we nearly forced a replay. Two late goals killed us off, but Marwood, McClaren and co. had done themselves proud, and it had been a thankless task up front for Keith Edwards, playing as a lone striker … with Nick Deacy.

Hull City were massively inferior to Spurs in every way 27 years ago, but today the roles are reversed. We are third, and they are bottom, and one of their best players is one of our cast-offs. Fraizer must be wishing he'd stayed on board the City juggernaut.

Matchday Experience Total – 34 out of 50

THE KC STADIUM

Sunday 19th October 2008 – 3pm

Hull City 1-0 West Ham United

Accessibility – 8 out of 10

For most visitors, the KC Stadium is on the accessible side of Hull, and the route in along the A63 is relatively scenic compared to the rest of the East Riding, where the relief is as flat as a pancake. The ground is clearly sign-posted off the dual carriageway, although a crafty attempt is made to direct you towards the park and ride scheme. I prefer to drive further on to seek a space nearer the ground.

Ample parking can usually be found on a vast expanse of derelict land down Walton Street, but not this week, as the fair has come to town, and not just any old fair. The sixteen acres of cracked concrete and weeds have been occupied by Europe's largest travelling fair, and although it finished last night, it will still take a few days to dismantle the huge array of big wheels, carousels and stomach churning rides.

Fortunately, my local knowledge provides me with plenty of alternatives, and I end up in a favourite spot half way down Princes Avenue, handily placed for drinking facilities.

Facilities – 8 out of 10

The top end of Princes Ave has changed markedly in recent years, and it now hosts several pubs, coffee bars and restaurants, many of which come complete with an outdoor terrace on the wide pavements. There can't be too many occasions over the season where it is comfortable to quaff your drinks in Hull's invigoratingly fresh air, but I suppose it's a handy haven for the smokers.

On the corner with Spring Bank, stands the New Zoological, as opposed to the old one, which was flattened some years ago, shortly before it fell down of its own accord. The new version is an ideal pre-match venue, complete with big screens, decent grub and acres of space. It is welcoming to away fans, and today there is a fair smattering of claret and blue.

I'm on the lookout for Ian, my ticket provider. He has kindly offered me his season pass, as he will be living it up in a private box with his boss. This is great news for me, as I would now be half way back to Hertfordshire otherwise. The heightened demand for tickets means that you have to be very organised and very quick off the mark if you want to snap them up. Organisation is not my strong point.

I find him by the bar, and he trustingly hands over his full book of tickets, as we won't know which ticket number is required until we reach the turnstiles. This, I presume, is to reduce the risk of forgery, but surely, any forger worth his salt will just forge a whole book.

I only have time for one quick drink, as Ian needs to take full advantage of his freebies at the ground. Our walk to the stadium takes us past a number of stalls, selling the usual collection of scarves and flags, but is noticeable that Brazil flags have been added to the choice in support of fans' favourite, Geovanni. How things have changed since I started going back in 1971. The closest thing we had to a foreign import back then was Terry Neill.

Collectively, these stalls are probably more productive than the old club shop in Bunkers Hill used to be in the dying days of Boothferry Park. I seem to remember that it gradually shrank in size as the crowds dwindled, and towards the end, it only stocked a couple of signed pictures and a hat.

The present store under the East Stand is another marker of our rapid rise in fortunes. The range of merchandise available is a million miles away from the Boothferry days, but despite the magnificent choice of wares, my initial target is always the bookstand. Here, I can sneakily re-arrange the display so that my debut offering, *Away With the Tigers* can sit proudly in front of autobiographies from Chilton and Wagstaff. Sorry chaps, but I know you do the same.

The Stadium – 7 out of 10

The approach from the railway bridge next to the Hull Royal Infirmary must be as impressive as any in the Premier League. The view is unobscured and you can see the stadium in its entirety. I love the way that the larger West Stand peeps over the smaller East Stand, giving a glimpse of the oval interior.

When first opened in 2002, many felt that the 25,000 capacity was wildly optimistic, but every game is now a sell-out, and we are rapidly outgrowing it, as a new generation of fans are taking advantage of being born in a city with a successful football team (something I used to dream of). If we stay in the Premiership, the East Stand will have to rise up to match the West.

The winding pathway to the stadium may well provide an excellent view, but it provides little else. The rough pasture on either side surely offers an ideal site for more pre-match facilities, but as yet, it remains barren. There has been talk of a railway platform, but that is all it's been … talk. Hopefully, something will spring up in the coming years, apart from weeds.

Inside the ground, my seat (ok, Ian's seat) provides a good view. It places me in row X, just to the right of the half way line looking out at the fine West Stand, with its distinctive curved upper tier. I sat in a similar position for my first ever visit to the KC; a drab 1-0 win over Bristol Rovers in January 2003. I spent most of that game staring up at the surroundings, unable to believe that the Tigers were now residing in such an awesome home.

It's all relative though. Having visited St. James' Park, the Emirates and Wembley in the last few months, the KC is starting to look a little pokey.

The Match – 5 out of 10

The resident KCFM DJ, Steve Jordan, carries out his usual warm-up act before the game. This involves an excitable introduction to each stand, which all have to cheer wildly in return. He saves the East Stand for the grand finale, where he nearly bursts a gasket giving us our cue, so we feel compelled to cheer louder than the other three stands. Having completed his job, he retires to the tunnel to find some throat lozenges.

The players are now allowed to emerge, and they march towards the portable Barclays Premier League frame, which is stationed on the half way line. A game of 'Oranges and Lemons' then ensues, where the players are required to run beneath the Barclays sign, before peeling off (pardon the pun) towards their own fans for a final warm up.

This is about as good as it gets for the next hour, as there is very little excitement on the pitch. Noise levels rise whenever Craig Bellamy receives the ball and he is given some well deserved stick, not just for mis-cueing a couple of shots, but for being Craig Bellamy.

There is the usual banter between fans, but the Hammers are quieter than I'd expected. I saw them in action at Watford a couple of weeks ago and they had sung relentlessly through that one. The Carling Cup tie had come a few days after Watford had conceded a phantom goal against Reading, where rookie referee, Stuart Attwell, had decided to trust his blind linesman rather than his own eyes, and awarded a goal to Reading when the ball had clearly gone out for a corner. This led them to chant, '1-0, 1-0, 1-0…' after one of their shots hit the side netting, and later in the half they tried their luck with, 'Lino. Lino give us a goal…'

But today they seem subdued. All we get is a couple of renditions of Blowing Bubbles in broad Cockney accents, '…and loyke moy dreams thy fide and doy…'

It's no surprise when we reach half time goalless. Despite our incredible start to the season, we still haven't got wise to the fact that we really should be beating sides like West Ham at home. The fans around me seem happy with the dull first half display, and as I chat to Steve, an old school friend, at half time, we agree that a boring 1-0 win would be an acceptable outcome.

The second half begins, and it looks like both teams have taken a bit of a half time bollocking. Within five minutes, City are in the lead. A corner swings in from Dawson's cultured left foot, and the imperious Turner heads home. What a player he has turned out to be. And to think, he was left out of the side for the first game of last season, a 3-2 home defeat to Plymouth, losing out to Danny Coles.

We then get ten minutes of end-to-end action. City break again and nearly add a second, then Carlton Cole hits our bar, but the pedestrian pace is gradually restored.

We look quite comfortable, until Phil Brown decides to defend the lead by taking off Geovanni and Cousin, leaving just a knackered Marlon King up front. It strikes me that we may be asking for trouble here, but the Hammers look short of ideas, and we hold firm.

Character – 6 out of 10

The stadium is very modern, but some distinctive design features give it some points. The two-tiered West Stand is a great sight, and the floodlights on top of the east side remind me of the old Wembley.

There is never any shortage of characters in the crowd, but my favourite today is a chap that I have come across before, three years ago at Crystal Palace. He is a southerner who used to support QPR, but he moved north and adopted the Tigers. I got stuck next to him in a pub near Selhurst Park and I got the life story. He is also a fierce patriot, but people can work that one out for themselves today, thanks to his t-shirt. A flag of St. George adorns the front, and on the back it reads:

'Proud to be English.

Not European,

Not British

F***ing English.'

I'm sure his strong feelings are temporarily suspended when City's starting eleven is announced. Only four Englishmen are in it.

Summary

The headlines had already been written before the game.

'London 0 Hull 4.'

The prophetic title of the Housemartins 1984 album summed up the story of our season so far. Four victories over London clubs in the first six weeks: Fulham, Arsenal, Spurs and West Ham. It's hard to believe.

Matchday Experience Total – 34 out of 50

THE HAWTHORNS

Saturday 25th October 2008 – 3pm

West Bromwich Albion 0-3 Hull City

Accessibility – 9 out of 10

The 'Cousins McGeown,' from Hampshire, will accompany me today. Stephen is an early riser. He likes to be up with the lark to pound the pavements in his running gear. Tomorrow he will be participating in the Great South Run in Portsmouth. He arrives bright and early.

Michael is the antithesis of Stephen. He has had an extremely heavy night on the lash and is handicapped by a major hangover. He has only had four hours sleep, but somehow, he also arrives early.

The journey up the M1 and M6 is trouble free except for an unscheduled stop at Corley Services, where a pale green Michael makes a bolt for the toilets. Whatever happens in there, it seems to do the trick and he is talking in positive terms about food by the time we reach West Bromwich.

The ground is well sign-posted off Junction 1 of the M5 and we are spoilt for choice with parking facilities. Mind you, it's still only midday and some of the attendants have not yet taken up their posts. We find a large car park close to the ground and choose a space right by the exit, ready for a quick getaway.

Facilities – 5 out of 10

We meet up with the McAllisters at the club shop, where Dennis Smith is signing copies of his autobiography. Well, he would be if anyone were queuing to buy it. The lack of takers is probably because he spent his entire playing career with Stoke City, and only 18 unsuccessful months as West Brom manager, before he was sacked.

The search for food begins, but the McDonalds opposite is not an option; Martin has already got himself barred. He only went in for an innocent Jimmy Riddle, but an over-officious manageress, who needs to brush up on customer relations, followed him into the toilets and informed him that he couldn't use the facilities unless he was buying food. He assured her that he actually *was* going to buy something, but he certainly *wouldn't* be now, which of course was a complete lie, but he had to try and save face.

With the only obvious food outlet ruled out, our search spreads further afield. Numerous mobile burger and hot dog vans decorate the roadsides, but a bitterly cold northerly breeze is blowing, and I don't relish the idea of standing out in it for the next couple of hours. It's unusually cold for mid October, and I fancy it may be partly due to our height above sea level. The Hawthorns is apparently the highest football league ground in the country, at 168 metres. Okay, it's not exactly on a mountain top, but there is a definite feeling today of being exposed to the elements.

The locals advise us to look for 'The Vine,' which accommodates away fans. This turns out to be well on the way to Wolverhampton, and the thirty-minute walk through the chilly wind rather defeats the object of looking for somewhere warm. When it is eventually found, I feel like Captain Scott when he saw that Amundsen had beaten him to the South Pole. The small inadequately equipped pub is overflowing with City fans, and the queue for the bar is stretching back out of the front door. Hunger rules our hearts and we all head for the nearest burger van.

Wherever you are in West Bromwich, you are never more than ten feet away from a burger van. They're everywhere, but they are all doing great business as there are no pubs around, and McDonalds is empty because of the mad manageress.

Our only option now is to head for the ground to get a drink, but of course, the City fans that are not in 'The Vine,' have all had the same idea. I've never had to stand in such cramped conditions inside the bar area at any ground. A couple of TV screens are showing the early kick off between Sunderland and Newcastle, which keeps me occupied, while Michael and Stephen enjoy a 25 minute queue for the bar. Michael comes back with his second burger of the day, and the hair of the dog. He's feeling better.

The Stadium – 7 out of 10

A small door is open at the side of the main stand in Halfords Lane. In large letters above, it reads; 'The Tony Brown Entrance.' Now, I know that Tony is a bit of a cult hero in these parts, having scored 279 goals for the club, but to provide him with his very own entrance?

The stadium looks quite promising at first glance, and four floodlight pylons are quite prominent as they stretch up from the roof and lean out over the pitch.

It is a nice compact ground inside. It holds 28,000, but the main stand is a little disappointing in size compared to the other three sides. A rebuild would be impossible with Halfords Lane running along the back of it, and Tony Brown would have to find another entrance.

The other three stands rise up to a far greater height and the corners have been partially filled in with a tier of seats. Above these, large corrugated metal sheets have been erected to create a fully enclosed arena. Two corners contain big screens, but the northeast corner is the resting place for a large throstle, sitting on top of a football.

Throstle, is the Black Country name for the thrush, which used to nestle in the hawthorn bushes of this region, hence, the nickname, the Throstles, and the home ground, the Hawthorns. Yet, strangely, a more common nickname has taken over – the Baggies. I say strangely, because no one really knows how it came about, though many theories abound. Some say it was down to baggy shorts that the team used to wear at the turn of the century: others say it is from protective trousers that factory workers wore in the area, or maybe it is derived from the bag men who used to collect the money at the turnstiles. Whatever the explanation, it sounds daft. They should stick with the Throstles.

The Match – 8 out of 10

The Baggies / Throstles (delete as applicable) come 'flying' out of the traps and it takes City a while to adjust to the pace of the game. Phil Brown must be blamed here for failing to take the squad away for some mid-week altitude training. The best chances fall to West Brom, with Roman Bednar striking the bar, and Ishmael Miller forcing Myhill into a fingertip save.

A fine atmosphere is being generated by the two sets of fans who are sharing the Smethwick End, although the opposition need the assistance of an irritating drummer to help generate some of the songs.

Miller gets a kick in the temple and returns with a bright white bandage wrapped around the top of his head. A witty chap behind me tries desperately to start up a song which points out Miller's resemblance to a pint of Guinness, but no one dares to join in for fear it could be construed as racist.

Half time arrives, and a couple of thousand fans simultaneously head for the solitary exit. Unsurprisingly, they reach total gridlock. I stay put.

The Tigers begin the second half well, their lungs having acclimatised to the thin mountain air, and it only takes us three minutes to take the lead. Zayatte, the discovery of the season so far, volleys in from a corner and quickly disappears under a heap of City players. Meanwhile, at the top of the stand, my celebration involves losing a mobile phone from my pocket and smacking my knee on the seat in front. It's worth the pain though.

Things just keep getting better from here on. Geovanni scores a diving header, just to prove that he doesn't only score thirty-yard screamers, and then Marlon King breaks away to slot in a third.

Football fans dream of moments like these. We are 3-0 up, away from home, with 20 minutes left to gloat, and we've got every right to, as we're about to go top of the Premiership. Well, technically we'll be third on goal difference, unless we score another thirteen, but it's not going to stop us singing about it all the way to the final whistle.

The Baggies are taunted, the drummer is taunted, and even Mark Lawrenson is taunted as he dared to predict on Football Focus that our bubble would burst today. We then get completely carried away and taunt Chelsea, our next opponents, which could be tempting fate a little.

It's all too much for the West Brom fans, who stream out in their droves with a sixth of the game remaining. I'm sure the KC Stadium would never empty in such premature fashion if we were three down. Maybe we'll find out next week.

Character – 6 out of 10

The surroundings are quite spacious and modern. The hawthorn bushes and throstles are long gone. There are lots of car parks and fields in the area, and the new Sandwell Academy takes up a few acres across Halfords Lane. This is a 'state of the art' school, specialising in sport and business enterprise, and it is very much supported by the football club who act as sponsors and governors.

I like the inside of the Hawthorns though. It is neat and tidy and the Throstle perched high in the corner is a nice touch. I hope that the Throstle nickname does not become obsolete. I would hate to see the ball and the bird replaced by a washing line and a pair of baggy shorts.

Summary

It has been a memorable day. A large share of the calls on Five Live's 606 phone-in relate to Hull City. It seems that we are the nation's second favourite team, and rightly so. We have taken the Premiership by storm, playing good football, and we have accrued 20 points from nine games.

Michael is still buzzing from today's game as we head back down the M1, and he declares that he's scared to go to another away game, because it can't get any better than this.

Maybe, but then I thought the same after Wembley, Newcastle, Arsenal and Tottenham.

Matchday Experience Total – 35 out of 50

Old Trafford

Saturday 1st November 2008 – 3pm

Manchester United 4-3 Hull City

Accessibility – 7 out of 10

This will be the most expensive match of the season, but only a small fraction of the outlay will be down to the football. It is my wife's birthday today, and an excursion to Old Trafford was not very high on her wish list. Patsy's compensation package, though, includes a six-hour shopping trip to the ridiculously huge and extravagantly ornate Trafford Shopping Centre. Extra pressure will be placed on the credit card with the presence of my three children who can all be very persuasive, and six hours is more than enough time to pester her into submission.

The Centre is easy to find off Junction 9 of Manchester's ring road, the M60, and it is only a short drive from here to Old Trafford. Several match day parking signs have been erected on the kerbsides directing visitors into a selection of car parks. I choose the first one that I see, on the supposition that it will be easier to escape back to the shopping centre after the game. The only drawback with this is the long twenty-minute walk to the ground. I pass several more empty car parks on the way and regret that I may have been a little hasty with my choice.

Facilities – 8 out of 10

I phone Gary, an old school chum, and we arrange to meet in the *Throstle's Nest*, even though he hasn't got a clue where it is. I decide to get to the ground and then ask for directions from there. The pub name worries me a little, though. I hope Gary realises that the West Brom match was two weeks ago.

The route to the stadium takes me past countless food stands, frying up a tempting range of greasy delights. Particularly eye-catching, are the one-foot long hot dogs (that's 30cm in newspeak) but I resist and hold out for the grub in the pub, if I ever find it.

Outside the club shop (sorry… megastore) I approach a policeman for directions to the *Throstles' Nest*. He replies in broad Geordie, and suggests that I should try asking a local steward as most of the police have been drafted in from Newcastle. His advice is taken, and I find an official-looking chap nearby with a ruddy complexion and a vacant stare. He looks like he enjoys a drink or two, and sure enough, he is able to provide precise directions, even though the pub is quite a way off; 25 minutes by his reckoning.

His estimate turns out to be pretty accurate, but only if you run all the way, which I practically do, so I'm wringing with sweat by the time I arrive at the 'Nest.' The pub is spacious with plenty of available seating, probably because it is so far from the ground that no sensible fans will even consider it. Not much is on offer in the way of pub grub, so once again, lunch is deferred.

Instead, we down a couple of beers before starting the long walk back to the ground, where I have arranged to pick up my 'borrowed' pass for the North Stand from Ben, an ex house-mate from the college days, who now lives in Warrington. I'm a bit edgy because we are running late, and I'm worried that he will find it hard to resist the advances of several Tiger chancers who are wandering around advertising their willingness to pay top dollar for any spare tickets, so there is no time to stop for a burger.

The Stadium – 9 out of 10

Ben is waiting faithfully in the prescribed meeting place, under a bronze statue of Sir Matt Busby. The 'Old Man' (Busby, not Ben) is staring across the road at another famous statue – one of Best, Law and Charlton. This site is a hotbed of photographic activity and Ben must have appeared in the background on a fair number of snaps during his wait.

To reach our turnstile, we need to walk under the first part of the 'Munich Tunnel,' which runs underneath the North Stand. We don't go down far enough to see all the plaques and photos that commemorate the lost babes of 1958, but I got the full low-down yesterday on an official stadium tour. The tour was an inclusive part of Patsy's birthday weekend package and it was a real treat for the whole family; at least I think it was. It took in the changing rooms, tunnel, dugouts, players' lounge and museum. Stephen, of course, lapped it up, as he has now well and truly sold his soul to the Red Devils for all eternity, but my teenage daughters, Elizabeth and Emma, are starting to take a healthy interest in Hull City's new-found notoriety. They happily joined me in the away dugout to test out Phil Brown's seat, not that he ever sits down much.

Craftily, the final stage of the tour brought us out through a secret exit, straight into the clutches of the megastore, where Stephen persuaded us to part with substantial sums of cash. Eight tills were in operation, but a small maze containing an additional forty checkouts was on standby ready for the matchday rush.

Talking of the matchday rush, Ben and I need to move pretty sharpish up a number of flights of stairs if we are not to miss kick off, so there is no time for a burger. Our seats are on the second tier, opposite the raised brick-built dugouts. We overlook the corner flag in the southeast corner; the City fans do likewise in the southwest corner. Considering that Old Trafford holds 76,000 people, the small allocation of 3,000 for away fans appears woefully inadequate, but at least they are treated to the best view, staring across at the two biggest stands. If I had been sitting amongst the City faithful, the stadium might have been given full marks, but my view of the west stand is not so impressive.

The Match – 10 out of 10

If there is one thing we must not do, it is to concede an early goal, so the omens are not good when Ronaldo finds the back of the net after barely three minutes resistance. Actually, the ball doesn't hit the back of the net, because it pings off the inside of the post and flies across goal, just over the line to the inside of the opposite side netting. That Ronaldo guy doesn't half score some fluky goals.

Ben leaps for joy, even though his football allegiance has taken more twists and turns than a Ronaldo dribble. He was brought up to support Blackpool, defected to Old Trafford, then switched to the Reebok to support his Bolton-born wife, but now he is making secret excursions to Anfield to placate his Liverpool-loving son. I'm sure I can turn him into a Tiger yet.

Red shirts surge forward with every attack and we look distinctly vulnerable. Just ten minutes have elapsed, and I find myself willing the digital display on the scoreboard to speed on towards half time, but it gives the impression of slowing rather than quickening. I suspect that Fergie may have a remote control for it.

Eventually, after 23 minutes, we win a dodgy free kick, and Marney's whipped cross is glanced in by Daniel Cousin, a man who saves his goals for the big stage. He runs off to the corner to milk the applause of the delirious Tigers' fans. Well, who wouldn't?

One of Manchester United's training ground drills must be to shoot across the keeper to score off the inside of a post, because three minutes later, they do it again. This time Carrick performs the trick, or is it just another fluke?

Now, if there is one thing that we must not do, it's concede before half time, but right on cue, with the fourth official holding up the board for two extra minutes, Ronaldo strikes again, nodding in a corner. Killer!

I try to console myself by heading for the food kiosks, but the queues are just silly, and it looks like they've run out of hot food anyway. I'm bloody starving, but I'll have to wait until after the game.

The second half gets under way, and if there is one thing that we mustn't do, it's let Man Utd score the next goal. Vidic gets it, unmarked from a corner. I hold my breath and prepare for the floodgates to open.

Despite the bleak outlook, City's fans maintain the singing.

'We support our local team,' they continually bellow, which is the ideal weapon to silence the Stretford End, as they can't join in. Blackpool-born Ben goes quiet too. On yesterday's tour, the guide asked the fifty-strong party, how many were going to the game. Most replied in the affirmative, but when asked how many were from Manchester, not one hand was raised. He conceded that most of the locals support Manchester City.

Phil Brown then pulls off a tactical masterstroke by bringing on Bernard Mendy, and United can't cope with his pace. First he scores, and then he wins a penalty after making Rio Ferdinand look like he was running in custard. Geovanni dispatches the kick, and suddenly, it's 4-3, there are ten minutes left, and United are pooing in their pants. Rooney shows his frustration and is lucky not to get sent off, which is pretty much like every other game he plays in.

Fergie presses fast forward on his remote, and the clock ticks round to the ninetieth minute. The whistle sounds. United are mightily relieved and we are mightily proud. Admittedly, we have been second best for most of the game, but we damn near nicked a point.

Character – 8 out of 10

Old Trafford is full of history, and by joining the stadium tour, I have been privileged to walk the corridors underneath the south stand, which should be able to share a host of memories of past glories. One corridor in particular should be more forthcoming than the others; the players tunnel, between the dugouts, which is the only section to have survived after the ground was flattened by German bombs. New stands were built after the war, but United had to share with Manchester City until 1949, which must have hurt.

The other disaster that is hard to avoid is the Munich air crash, and a fair percentage of the museum is devoted to this. The 1958 disaster is a major reason why so many neutrals adopted United as their team over the years, and I can understand why. It is quite a sobering experience, standing in the museum, reading the original newspaper reports, listening to the radio broadcasts, and watching footage of the great Duncan Edwards. I always wonder how much Edwards might have achieved had he survived. He was always rated more highly than Bobby Charlton, and Bobby didn't turn out too bad did he?

Summary

It's our 6th outing in the Premiership, and our first defeat, but at least we didn't concede our unbeaten away record without a fight. We scored three times at Old Trafford, and were even awarded a penalty in front of the Stretford End. Visitors can rarely make such claims.

Matchday Experience Total – 42 out of 50

FRATTON PARK

Saturday 22nd November 2008 – 3pm

Portsmouth 2-2 Hull City

Accessibility – 7 out of 10

Thirty years ago, Chris and I would meet regularly on the crumbling Kempton terraces, but today, we will be reunited at a crumbling Fratton Park. He now lives in Emsworth, a charming village just a few miles along the coast from Portsmouth, which is a far cry from his native Orchard Park.

His inside knowledge of the local area has influenced my travel plan, and we have agreed on a midday meeting at Havant Station. I'm quite happy about this, as it saves driving blindly into the heart of Portsmouth, where parking spaces are apparently in short supply, and a quick getaway would be out of the question.

It takes only an hour and a half to make it down the M25 and A3, and there are plenty of spaces at Havant Station. The combined cost of parking and the three-stop return to Fratton is just five pounds. Good value, as it's a fact of football life nowadays that you'll be stung for at least a fiver at any ground for parking. From Fratton Station, the floodlight pylons are clearly visible, but a ten-minute walk is still ahead of us.

I'm worried about getting the train back after the game, and my worst fears are realised at 5 o'clock when we arrive at a chock-a-block platform. Trains are meant to leave every ten minutes, but with so many bodies squashed in front of us, I can't realistically see us boarding anything for the next half hour.

Yet, incredibly, when the automatic doors slide open on the Havant-bound express, everyone stands like statues, and we are able to squeeze through the masses to take our seats in a half empty carriage. It strikes us immediately that they may all have heard something about Havant that we haven't, and we wait anxiously for an announcement telling us that the next stop is a far-flung coastal town like Dover, but no, it just seems that they all want the local line. Our train is due to branch off to Waterloo after Havant. Phew!

Facilities – 5 out of 10

Chris has taken advice from the locals on the best places to drink. Most pubs are for home fans only, so we head past the ground to Milton Road, where there are a couple of possibilities. The first option is the Brewers Arms, and we take it. The choice is not based on any detailed survey of facilities, but because we're cold. It doesn't offer much in the way of food, but we're able to grab a seat, and a couple of beers, and we can watch the lunchtime football on Sky; not much more a man can ask for really.

Eventually, we are driven on by hunger, and the fact that we may miss the kick off. We march briskly to the ground, where we will be sitting in the Portsmouth half of the Milton Stand. The first thing that we see upon stumbling through the turnstile is a ramshackle hut and a large queue. A variety of hot and cold snacks are being served from a hatch, and the whole operation is being run by two people, possibly a husband and wife team, and they are struggling to cope with demand. It is close to kick off before Chris and I can finally satisfy our hunger by biting into a hotdog.

Just to the side of the hut, there are two doors; a ladies and a gents. Hardly adequate, I would doubt, for the two thousand fans on this side of the stand. Apparently, these basic amenities are mirrored on the opposite corner for the City fans. Premier League?

Stadium – 5 out of 10

Two of the stands are completely hemmed in by housing. We eat our hot dogs at the back of the Milton End, staring down into the neighbour's back gardens, and we can virtually watch the television sets through their patio windows. This might actually be necessary at half time, as there are no flat screens around to keep us updated with other matches on Sky Sports News.

Directly below us, between the stand and the garden fences, there runs a narrow tenfoot, although we must not refer to it as such, lest we should give away our East Riding roots, not that anyone will have a clue what we're talking about. City fans are streaming out of the pubs now, along the ten foot wide alley, hoping to make it in time for the start. I just hope they've eaten.

An earlier circumnavigation of the ground revealed that the Fratton Park dilapidation is evenly spread. The club are well aware of this fact, and numerous ideas have been floated to move them into the 21st century. One scheme literally did try to 'float' a new stadium by suggesting building it out into the harbour, but the location was next to a large shopping centre and the potential Saturday congestion means that it is now 'dead in the water.'

Another plan was to remain on the same site, but rotate the stadium 90 degrees. It is highly likely that this idea has been shelved as well, because my slightly out of date guide to Premiership grounds predicts that it should be completed by 2006.

The latest plan is to build on a site out of town. The city certainly needs something more befitting of a Premiership side, and it could give the club the boost that it needs. Just look at how it helped Southampton!

Chris and I polish off our hot dogs, and find Section Q at the top of the stand. We are directed to our seats behind the goal, which are fine in the way of location, but not in the way of comfort. Leg room was not taken into account when these were bolted into the concrete, and Chris' 6ft 6in frame is going to experience an uncomfortable ninety minutes. I detect a look of envy in his eye as he watches Peter Crouch frolic freely around the field like a frisky newborn foal.

The City fans are to our right, and so is the big screen in the corner, although the bottom of it is obscured slightly by the roof of another run-down shed-like structure. To our left, we have the 'Pompey Bandstand,' where a motley collection of creatures are setting themselves up to irritate the hell out of everyone for the entire match with a range of drums, bells, whistles and hooters: hardly a band.

The Match – 7 out of 10

Portsmouth begin the brighter, with an early header from 'Utaka the attacker' crashing against the bar, before bouncing down on the line. To our great relief, the referee waves 'play on,' so all eyes turn to the big screen for a replay, but infuriatingly, the crucial bounce disappears behind the top of the police hut that supports the screen.

The bandstand then comes to life. I'm not quite sure what they're trying to achieve with their relentless rhythmless pounding, but it doesn't provide any cues for the Pompey fans to break into song, in fact, if anything, it's a complete distraction. Chris tells me that they used to be stationed at the opposite end of the ground. I'll bet there was great rejoicing down there when it was finally shifted, and great misery up here. No one seems to want it, but it would take a brave man to tell the gruesome bell-ringing leader of the band to shift his great sweaty tattooed carcass and shove his bell where the sun don't shine.

The home crowd needs little encouragement to sing, though, when Crouch heads them into the lead with a typical towering header. Turner and Zayatte are in for a torrid afternoon if the ball keeps finding Crouch's head.

It takes a while, but City gradually gain some possession and work their way into the match, and just before the break, we nearly level from a 30-yard Geovanni wonder strike. Only Geo would expect to succeed from such a range, but this effort narrowly fails, pinging off the angle of bar and post.

Despite the increasing pressure on the Portsmouth goal, I'm forced to nip out early to the toilet, not due to a bulging bladder, but because it might be my only chance. It proves to be a wise decision, as the solitary facility operates reverse technology to the Tardis – it's smaller on the inside than the outside. The half time whistle goes as I exit, and I'm nearly swept back through the door by the stampede of desperate fans, who just about managed to hold it until the break.

Early in the second period, Chris tunes into the comments in the home end, and keeps reporting them back to me, as if I can't understand the local lingo.

'They're going to score. I can see it coming,' one of our neighbours fears. He's dead right. Our pressure pays off when Turner heads in from a corner.

We sense fear and go for the kill. Marney brings out a great save from David James (still England's number one, by default) and the locals are starting to fret. The ground is suddenly eerily quiet, then I realise why. The band has temporarily put its booming and clanking on hold. Chris is able to tune in again to the home fans' wavelength.

'We're going to get turned over here,' they agree.

But Glenn Johnson has other ideas, and he turns the game on its head with a terrific dipping volley from outside the box. Myhill can only stand in admiration as his fizzing shot nestles in the top corner, and suddenly, Fratton Park is rocking again, including the bleedin' bandstand.

Utaka the attacker nearly seals it shortly afterwards, but he looks more like Utaka the defender when he spoons the ball over from 3 yards.

Then Deano comes on. The game is set up perfectly for him: 2-1 down with barely ten minutes left, and sure enough, he is soon running the length of the pitch with his arms aloft after applying the vital touch at the end of a goalmouth scramble.

'DEANO! DEANO!'

Boy, it feels good to be singing that again.

It's another creditable away point, and we hang around after the final whistle to watch replays on the big screen. It looks like the winner may have come off Pamarot, although Deano did get a faint touch. One thing's for sure though: Deano will claim it, and I'm sure Pamarot doesn't want it.

Character – 7 out of 10

The old-style floodlight pylons always help to add a splash of character, and they remind me of bygone days at Boothferry Park, although Portsmouth can only manage four; we had six. Hah!

The gantry for the TV cameras in the Carisbrook Road Stand also evokes memories of our former home. Commentators and cameramen need a steady head for heights if they are to negotiate the rickety walkway that leads to their exposed position in the roof. I'm sure Motty brings the old sheepskin coat out of the mothballs for winter visits to Fratton Park.

If you're a fan of 'Life on Mars,' and you are nostalgic about the seventies, then you'll love this ground.

What are you waiting for? Get on those flares; tie a scarf to your wrist; head for the Milton End, and join the queue for Bovril at a dodgy shed.

Summary

Five days later, Portsmouth play AC Milan in the UEFA Cup and achieve another 2-2 draw. Milan leave it even later than City, scoring twice in the last ten minutes, so you might argue that we did better than Milan. It's another indicator of our progress. Not only are we one of the best teams in England at present, but Europe too.

Matchday Experience Total – 31 out of 50

THE BRITANNIA STADIUM

Saturday 29th November 2008 – 3pm

Stoke City 1-1 Hull City

Accessibility – 6 out of 10

The Stoke City website lied. It said that the Britannia Stadium was 'clearly visible' from the A50. It had not accounted, though, for the pea soup blanket of fog that has descended today on Staffordshire. *Nothing* is visible from the A50!

A small white sign appears out of the mist, suggesting that I might like to exit for the stadium, but it is too late; I'm already speeding past the junction in the outside lane, and a sharp yank to the left on the steering wheel at this stage would surely cause a pile up. The faint silhouette of a football stadium can just be made out on the opposite side of the dual carriageway. Bugger.

What can be more irritating than missing a turning and driving for miles in the wrong direction? How about, missing a turning, driving for miles, and joining a traffic jam. A chain of brake lights turn the fog a luminous red as the two lanes grind to a halt. An extra twenty pointless minutes are added to the journey time before I can finally double back and locate the handily placed Harvester Restaurant, opposite the ground.

Thanks to the delay on the A50, I've missed out on their parking spaces, but more are available next door at the Holiday Inn. The attendants at the entrance ask me if I'm a guest at the hotel, but my brain is none too sharp after the long journey. I instinctively provide an honest answer and pass up the opportunity to enjoy free parking. Six pounds is today's criminal going rate. They've got you over a barrel these match day car parks.

Facilities - 7 out of 10

The Harvester is an obvious meeting place for both sets of fans, which explains the long queue outside. Two bouncers are regulating a slow flow through the door, and another beefy chap is guarding the beer garden gate, to prevent gatecrashers, literally.

It's a struggle to get anywhere near the bar, but fortunately, I've timed my entrance to perfection, as cousin Hugh is already there, and within two minutes of arriving, I have a refreshing beer in my hand.

It's an equally challenging struggle to get away from the bar; such is the crush of bodies. We squeeze out to the well-protected beer garden, where unsurprisingly, Hugh's family have claimed an empty table. The beer is cold, the bench is frosty, and the fog is freezing; I've had more relaxing drinks.

A programme seller then hurdles the low fence and sets up a temporary stall on the neighbouring table. I've seen programmes being sold *in* grounds, *outside* grounds and *near* grounds, but never in a pub. He drums up a good trade, including three pounds from my pocket, before trying his luck inside. The front cover displays the familiar face of Leon Cort. If this is an attempt to wind us up, it won't work. Cort's sale was a good bit of business, and his replacement, Michael Turner, has been a Premier League revelation.

After flicking through the pages, my fingers are displaying the early symptoms of frostbite, so I visit the gents to thaw out. It is a relief, in more ways than one. The toilets are warm, roomy, clean and fragrant; an ideal place, in fact, to bring our beer. I give the idea serious consideration, before deciding that Michele may not be welcome.

Plan B is to visit the Stoke City shop. By the time we reach it, we are well and truly chilled to the bone, so the warm blast of air that hits me in the face at the entrance is most welcome. I have minimal interest in the broad range of Stoke merchandise, but the same cannot be said for my sad relatives. Hugh has been collecting mugs from each Premiership club, while Joe has developed a cushion fetish, but these are not so easy to come by. His favourite so far is his Portsmouth cushion, which was decorated with the home colours on one side, and away colours on the other. Don't ask me what he does with them.

All too soon, we are back out in the cold, taking evasive action as Craig Fagan's tank of a car mounts the pavement to roll up at a set of private gates. Martin and Joe immediately regress to childhood and chase after him to collect an autograph. By running round the corner, they are able to hand their programme through some railings, allowing Craig to scribble indiscriminately on the front cover, right across Leon Cort's face. At first, Martin thinks he's just testing the pen to see if it works, but no, this actually is his autograph. A second random squiggle is produced on Joe's programme, nothing like the first. He can't even forge his own signature.

Onwards to the turnstiles. A large burger stand, stands in the way, and I can't resist, but I'll have to eat it quickly, because my hands are numb again. Did I mention that it's cold? I could wear gloves, of course, but I don't believe in wearing them for football matches, as it muffles the clapping, equivalent to singing with a sock in your mouth.

Inside, there is plenty of space in the generously sized holding bay for City fans, although most of them appear to be waiting until the last second before venturing out into the icy late November air.

The Stadium – 6 out of 10

The Britannia Stadium is still relatively new. It hosted its first game in 1997, at a time when most other clubs preferred to rebuild existing stands rather than to relocate. Lots of clubs have followed suit since, though, including the Tigers, and as with most new grounds, the Britannia provides liberal amounts of space on the outside for those who like to circumnavigate. That would be me.

It is immediately noticeable that wide-open gaps exist on three corners of the ground. I have a theory for this. The grass type on the Britannia pitch must require natural sunlight, as the only enclosed corner is in the sunless northeast. Otherwise, surely they would fill the corners with seats to raise the capacity above the present 28,000. Such redundant spaces would also be ideal for a couple of big screens, but they don't have any. They don't even have a scoreboard, although I distinctly remember taking a photo of one last time I visited, when we were 3-0 up.

The fog continues to roll in as kick off approaches, and the far goal is barely visible. I pray that it doesn't get any worse. I don't fancy returning for a mid-week rearrangement.

The Match – 6 out of 10

The result of this game will hinge on our ability to deal with Rory Delap's world famous long throws, but only five are hurled in during the first half, and we cope with them well. It appears to be their only threat, and the home fans know this, hence their great excitement whenever we concede a throw.

Each club has been forced to develop anti-Delap strategies, and today, the Tigers have come up with a couple of truly original ideas. Firstly, Myhill opts to hoof the ball out for a corner, rather than give Delap the pleasure, and then Mr. Windass exercises his right to warm up on the touchline, irritatingly close to Rory as he prepares for another Howitzer. Our man receives a warning on the first one, but gets a booking when he tries it again. Only Deano would have the nerve to attempt such a stunt.

It's a game of few genuine chances, but on the stroke of half time, City break the deadlock. A mystery player plants a lovely shot into the top corner, but the fog prevents me from identifying the scorer. No one around me seems sure either, so I rely on the wonders of modern technology by texting my brother in Spain. He confirms that it was Marlon King.

Play continues in the same vein in the second half until Delap finally finds Fuller's head with a low flat missile, and Myhill pulls off a commendable reflex save to his right.

The atmosphere in the ground is something to behold. It's not often that our travelling support gets drowned out, but these Stoke fans are a rowdy lot. Credit here, where credit is due. I've been to Old Trafford, the Emirates and St. James' so far this season, but the atmosphere today beats them all by a country mile, and it's not even a great game.

Spurred on by this, they eventually force an equaliser. Fuller races clear and nicks the ball ahead of Myhill before hitting the deck. The crowd spurs the ref on too, and he points to the spot. Memories of our 2006 victory come flooding back. Myhill saved two penalties on that occasion, at the same end. He comes agonisingly close to repeating the feat, getting a strong hand on Fuller's strike, but it squeezes in.

Most of the excitement in the closing stages involves throw-ins and towels. Each time Delap prepares to launch one, he takes the best part of a minute to dry the ball on a red towel handed to him by a colluding ball boy. Cheating? Maybe. Time-wasting? Certainly!

Surely, it would be no different if a shoe-shine boy ran on to assist Geovanni before he took a free kick. Nonetheless, the referee allows the dubious practice to continue, so the Tigers' players find their own way to take retribution. Sam Ricketts snatches one of the towels with two minutes remaining and uses it to dry the ball for his own Delap-style rocket into the Stoke box. It bounces loose and creates brief panic before they clear their lines. What sweet justice it would have been, if we'd scored with their secret weapon, after 'borrowing' one of their towels.

Paul McShane then repeats the trick, but he is just taking the piss. We are pinned back near our own corner flag, in the dying seconds, but even so, he grabs a towel and makes a real show of drying the ball, in his own good time, while the Stoke players have the balls to accuse him of time wasting. Then, just for good measure, he wipes his armpits and hair with it. Brilliant.

The whistle goes. It's been a poor game of football, yet somehow, hugely entertaining.

Character & Tradition – 6 out of 10

A few famous players have passed through the Stoke ranks over the years, none more so than Sir Stanley Matthews. A fine memorial statue has been erected on the far side of the main car park, depicting him in three bronze action poses, running across the surface of a huge cuboid concrete block. It looks like three stills from an animated sequence. The first shows him jinking to the right, the second has him dribbling onwards, and in the third, he's producing a shot.

Of course, the monument is a magnet for cameras, and Hugh is tempted to climb on top of the 8-foot high mounting to pose for a tackle on the great maestro. I wonder how the 'wizard on the wing' would view Stoke's current long ball and long throw policy. I'll bet he's swerving in his grave!

Another statue is spotted as we pass the glass-fronted entrance of the stadium. This one is of Gordon Banks, standing holding a ball. To me it looks incomplete. What it really needs is a statue of Ken Wagstaff slipping a couple of shots past him.

The ground itself is quite new and lacks character, and neither Matthews nor Banks ever got to play here. All of their achievements were gained at the old Victoria Ground, which is now a derelict site, awaiting a housing development. It's a shame really, because at the time of demolition in 1997, it was thought to be the oldest operational football ground in the world.

Summary

Thankfully, the fog cleared slightly in the second half. It's been a long time since we were abandoned for fog. Possibly, it was the 1971 home clash with Blackburn when we were 2-0 up at half time. I remember it well; I was there, and I'm still bitter about it, as the rearranged game ended in a frustrating 0-0 draw.

Matchday Experience Total – 31 out of 50

ANFIELD

Saturday 13th December 2008 – 3pm

Liverpool 2-2 Hull City

Paul Collingwood

Accessibility 6 out of 10

The modern day scourge known as corporate hospitality is frequently blamed for diluting the atmosphere at top grounds, and for minimising opportunities for the 'real fans' to lay their hands on tickets. Well, I consider myself to be a 'real fan' so I have no qualms about accepting an invitation to join a table of ten at Anfield for pre-match and post-match wining and dining.

We are determined to relish the day, so no one is driving. Train is the chosen mode of transport, the 8:30 departure from Paragon to be precise. Chris (the organiser of the whole shebang) and four others will meet us there, so I settle down into the reserved seats with Dave (Chris' brother), Ian, Steve and Steve's dad, who is 82 years young. His name is Peter, but I feel awkward calling a senior citizen by his first name, so I'll refer to him as Mr D. from here on.

A change is necessary at Manchester Piccadilly, and the connection is made without a hitch, except that the previous Liverpool train had been cancelled, so it's a bit cramped. Mr D. is offered a seat, but the rest of us stand, and the train crawls slowly on its way, stopping at most stations, making a complete mockery of its billing: the 'Trans-Pennine Express.'

Arrival at Liverpool prompts a mad dash for the taxi rank, but a long queue has already formed ahead of us, which wouldn't be so bad if any taxis were actually rolling up. Our destination, *Orry's Café Bar,* is apparently half an hour's walk away; an hour with Mr. D in tow, so any notion of trying to jog it from here is quickly dispelled. Also, it's teeming down with rain.

After ten minutes, a taxi finally swings in to the bay, but just one bloke at the head of the queue climbs in, and away it goes. Valuable drinking time is slipping away – that's drinking time from a free bar!

Encouragingly, a few people in the line lose patience, and head out into the perpetual Lancastrian drizzle, slightly reducing our wait. Three Hackney carriages then pull in together, and another significant step is taken forward.

A second gaggle of taxis then arrive (if that's the correct collective noun) and eventually, we are on our way to the bar. We get there for 12:30 and Chris is waiting. The corporate experience can begin.

Facilities – 10 out of 10

The early signs are hugely encouraging. We are shown upstairs to a private function room, where several circular tables have been immaculately prepared, each with ten place settings, wine glasses and name cards, exactly as you would expect to see at a wedding. A match programme has been neatly laid between each knife and fork as a final touch.

A choice of cold or hot foods is available at the free buffet, where the attentive chef dishes me up a delicious plate of lemon garlic chicken. Free bottles of wine are placed on each table, while the free match tickets are handed out. A waitress keeps taking our bar orders in case we want free beer instead of free wine. We really couldn't ask for much more, except maybe a 3-0 away win.

I receive a text from cousin Hugh, informing me that he has just arrived at the Shankly Gates. I reply back that I may have just passed through the Pearly Gates, because it feels like we're in heaven. Dave suggests that the train may have crashed on the way here, and we're all dead, but I don't remember seeing a man with a long white beard and halo at the door, named Pete, checking off names on a clipboard. Anyway, he would surely have turned us away and redirected us to the underworld.

Our empty plates are cleared away, and the entertainment begins. An archetypal Scouse comedian is the host, and he revels in some spontaneous banter with both sets of fans. He is actually quite funny, and very quick to put hecklers in their place, so I keep my head down.

He asks for a show of hands to discover how many people are visiting Anfield for the first time. Quite a number of us are, including one woman, who bravely admits that this will be her first football match ever. The comic appears to take a genuine interest in this.

'Actually,' he observes, 'there are a growing number of women attending Premiership football matches nowadays, and to tell you the truth, there is fuck all we can do about it.'

The room, which is 90% men, erupts with laughter, and she goes Liverpool red.

Next, John Aldridge is introduced, and we are treated to more banter and anecdotes from his playing days, including an absolute classic about the time his father decked the referee in the Boothferry Park changing room after John had been sent off playing for Newport.

It gets to 2.30pm and we suddenly remember that there is a game of football to go to, but no fear; a fleet of free taxis are waiting outside to ferry us to the game. It just gets better and better. We pile into a cab and our driver hands us his mobile number. We just have to phone him after the match and he will be waiting to whisk us back to the pub. Heaven surely can't be as organised as this.

He suggests, however, that we should all leave before stoppage time to beat the crowds. We agree in principle, but there is no way it is going to happen in practice. He'll just have to wait.

The Stadium – 8 out of 10

When you have just died and gone to heaven, you are granted certain privileges. One of these obviously provides our taxi driver with a licence to ignore 'road closed' signs and police cordons. As a consequence, we are dropped right outside the Shankly Gates, where everyone is busily taking the compulsory photos of the overhead lettering: 'You'll Never Walk Alone.'

It is hard to get a panoramic photo of the whole stadium though, as you can't take ten steps back without bumping into Coronation Street style housing. Further desired expansion of the ground is completely impossible, therefore, and the nearby Stanley Park has been suggested as a possible site for relocation. The credit crunch and internal boardroom divisions appear to have put the brakes on that pipe dream though.

All ten of us will be sitting together in the Main Stand, in amongst the Liverpool fans. Hopefully, the 'security in numbers' adage will ring true, for there is a strong possibility that one of our gathering will go bananas if City score.

The inside of the Main Stand is showing its age and it is rather cramped, so we head for the seats to take in the atmosphere. Dave and I stand and admire the scene for a while, still unable to quite believe that we belong in this company. Where would we be playing today I wonder, if we had lost in the Play-off Final. Doncaster? Barnsley? QPR maybe?

Fussy stewards eventually direct us to our seats, where the hard antique wooden flaps provide an uncomfortable welcome. Oh for the padded luxury of the Emirates.

The scoreboard in the opposite corner sends a tingle down the spine. The game has not kicked off yet, so obviously the score is 0-0, but just to see the names Liverpool and Hull City illuminated side by side at Anfield almost makes the trip worthwhile already. Then I get another tingle, as 'You'll Never Walk Alone' starts up, and the whole stadium seems to be raising their scarves above their heads in the traditional manner. We're in the Liverpool end so we join in, forgetting that our scarves are the wrong colour. All of the City fans to our left in the Anfield Road End are doing it too. It is a cracking pre-match atmosphere.

The Match – 8 out of 10

I don't know what Bernard Mendy has had for breakfast, but it can't be legal. He's like a man possessed, skinning the Liverpool defence alive at every opportunity. His blistering pace draws a rash tackle from Dossena, and the free kick almost sets up a header for Turner. Not to worry; the ball works its way out to King and he whips it in again. This time it's McShane who gets there first and his header loops over Pepe Reina.

Our earlier pledge to keep a low profile goes straight out of the window. All ten of us are off our seats, leaping about, hugging each other, and we don't give a shit. The Scousers around us must be highly irritated, but they tolerate the situation, believing that our joy will be short-lived. One-nil up at Anfield; it doesn't get much better than this, unless you go two up - and then we do.

Again, it comes from a mad Mendy dash down the right. He reaches the by-line before pulling it back into the six-yard box, but Jamie Carragher is waiting. Jamie Carragher, the England international defender with 34 caps, as solid as they come, but with no left foot apparently, for instead of routinely clearing with his left, he inexplicably tries to wrap his right foot around the ball, and comically diverts it into the empty net.

We're off the seats again, but our hosts are not so accommodating this time and a number of shell-shocked locals make strong suggestions that we should sit down.

Two-nil up at Anfield! This is getting really silly, and it's obvious that we *did* die in that train crash after all; otherwise, this is fast becoming the best day of my life. It's right up there with the play-off final, pushing the wedding day into 3rd place, and the birth of my children into 4th, 5th and 6th. Dave takes a photo of the scoreboard and texts it to me with the caption, 'How good is that?'

It's a good job he acted when he did, as Liverpool are soon back in it when Gerrard converts a Benayoun cross.

Then comes a key moment in the game, when McShane becomes concussed. His head is spinning and he's not too sure where he is, which is probably also an accurate description of the ten Hull City fans sitting in the Main Stand, and not just because of the alcohol. McShane is withdrawn, and the marauding Mendy fills in at right back, which must please Dossena no end. Dean Marney will not cause him the same trouble.

Liverpool are now on top, and Gerrard half-volleys in an equaliser. Sitting to my right is Ian, the eternal pessimist. 'We're going to get battered,' he cheerfully predicts. 'I can see it ending up 5-2.'

I counter this with my eternal optimism, forecasting that we will weather the present storm, before sneaking a late winner. We are both wrong.

The second half is no less entertaining, but we don't threaten the Kop End too often. The City fans are in Christmas party mode, and even adopt the charitable Band Aid anthem for a dig at the home fans: 'Feed the Scousers. Let them know it's Christmas time.'

Benitez must be feeling the Christmas spirit too, for he stubbornly refuses to bring on Robbie Keane, preferring the ineffective Lucas instead. Stoppage time arrives, and the cab driver will have to wait. A late winner would really put the icing on the Christmas cake, but it is not to be, and the wedding day jumps back up into second place.

Character – 8 out of 10

The Shankly Gates are a distinctive feature, but they are nothing to write home about. If you've seen one big set of iron gates, then you've seen them all.

The inside of the ground has seen better days. Horrible bum-numbing wooden seats could be replaced, and there are thick red iron girders everywhere, one of which partially restricts my view of the Kop End goalmouth. They may add some character, but they are bloody annoying.

Restricted view or not, the sight and sound of the Kop singing 'You'll Never Walk Alone' is something unique to football, and would have been worth the entrance fee alone - if I'd had to pay.

Summary

The festivities did not end at the final whistle. The taxis took us back to *Orry's Bar,* where the tables had been re-set for more food and drink. Did I tell you that it was all free?

It would have been the perfect day had we snatched the win, and we actually felt a little peeved on the journey home that we only got a draw. Phil Brown is not too happy either. Replays show that Michael Turner was pushed for both Liverpool goals, but you don't get decisions like that in front of the Kop.

Matchday Experience Total – 40 out of 50

Disgruntled Newcastle fans.

The impressive Jack Milburn Stand

WE ARE TOP DA LEAGUE - Stephen and me at West Brom

The 'United Trinity

Facilities at Portsmouth. Premiership?

Pompey sunset

Shankly Gates or Pearly Gates?

Spiral Walkways at Eastlands

St Luke the Evangelist, and its back garden

The Cottage, and its front garden

Stokoe - The Sunderland Messiah

The Holte End - Aston Villa

Michele steers the Tigers to safety

WE ARE STAYING UP!

THE CITY OF
MANCHESTER STADIUM

Friday 26th December 2008 – 3pm

Manchester City 5-1 Hull City

Paul Collingwood

Accessibility 6 out of 10

It is always difficult to judge the time of departure, but especially so today – Boxing Day. Will the roads be empty because of a nationwide hangover, or will the shoppers be out in droves hunting for bargains in the sales?

An extra hour needs to be added onto my journey time before I even set out, as Christmas Day was spent at brother Tony's in Wimbledon, so my calculations determine an eight o'clock start. That's seven hours until kick off; surely enough time.

Predictably though, I fail to leave at the planned hour. A delicate head, and an extended visit to the toilet, delay me by thirty minutes. The decision to come in two separate cars was a wise one. I don't think the other four family members would have been ready. I'm probably still over the legal limit for driving, but I'm soon careering around the M25, which is clear, even if my head is not.

A brief detour is needed through Hemel Hempstead, as I forgot to bring my ticket confirmation e-mail. I still need to collect the ticket at the ground, and I won't relax until it is safely tucked inside my jacket pocket.

Finally, I am able to shoot up the M6, which is easier said than done. Invariably, there will be some kind of hold up, and today's 'incident' is situated between junctions 16 and 17. Plenty of advanced warnings are given about this, on flashing overhead signs, but I go into denial, and irrationally decide that it will fail to materialise. But, materialise it does, in the form of a stationary jam, where most of my queuing compatriots find it economical to turn off their engines.

The trouble with jams is, you don't know how long you'll be stuck for. My imagination conjures up a major twenty car pile up, and I start to plan alternative routes, but just as I'm accepting missing part of the game, the traffic starts to flow again, gradually increasing in speed until we're all cruising at the national speed limit. Not a car crash in sight. Baffling!

Thankfully, the phantom incident has cleared in good time, and my new ETA is around the 2 o'clock mark. Signposting off the M56 is fairly good; I just need to head for Sport City.

As usual, I select the first car park that I see, and follow a few sky blue clad fans through an unfavourable housing estate, where most windows have been boarded up. I can't establish whether this is because they are derelict, or if it's just general practice around here. I jog through most of it; not because I am scared you understand, but because I'm anxious to get hold of that ticket.

Facilities – 10 out of 10

My quest for the ticket office takes me round half of the stadium. I'm extremely hungry, but several mobile food outlets with short queues will have to wait. Three separate club shops are passed too, but the main one is right opposite the ticket office. I join the queue, but I'm still nervous. Will my crumpled e-mail and reference number be sufficient for the young lads working in the hut? I was unable to purchase anything in the Tigers' end, so for the third time this season, I have been forced to join another club's membership scheme, enabling me to order a ticket in the Colin Bell Stand, amongst the locals.

I reach the front of the line, and step forward. The assistant accepts my printout and retreats to the back of the hut, where he fingers through a stack of white envelopes, arranged neatly in wooden trays. The longer he searches, the more I sweat. Maybe they sent it out in the Christmas post, and it's still sitting in the Manchester sorting office. Or, more likely, he's just pressed a red button under the counter, and he's stalling for time while security staff come to escort me out of town.

Bingo! He finds it, and a white envelope with my name on it is handed through the grill. I tear it open, like Charlie Bucket searching for the golden ticket in Charlie and the Chocolate Factory, except this one is sky blue. Relief!

Turnstile P is quickly located and I get inside. There is just enough time to inspect the plush and exceptionally spacious concourse that runs underneath the stand. There is a wide choice of kiosks and bars (very Wembley-like) except that the bars are all named after Manchester City legends of the 1970's era.

The first of these is the Mike Sumerbee Bar. He must be well pissed off that Colin Bell got a whole stand named after him rather than a small bar, although I'm sure he raises a vengeful laugh every time someone refers to Colin's stand as the 'Bell End.'

Next, is the Francis Lee Bar, where fittingly, a meal-deal consists of two Fosters and two pies for £10. Classy.

A little further on, I spy a third bar, and I make a few guesses in advance: Rodney Marsh maybe, or Joe Corrigan? No, it turns out to be the Colin Bell Bar. Well, that hardly seems fair. He gets a bar and a stand?

There are toilets a plenty, but these are not named after players, although I'm sure the long suffering Man City fans could think of some appropriate candidates.

The Stadium – 10 out of 10

The City of Manchester Stadium was built for the 2002 Commonwealth Games, and Manchester City moved in a year later. It is a fine piece of architecture. Several cylindrical columns are spaced around the exterior, providing spiral walkways for the fans in the upper tiers. This clever piece of design creates extra space inside, which is why the concourses are so wide, and well stocked with bars.

The 'Bell End' is not actually an end – it's a side – the west side of the ground. It is a magnificent three-tiered structure, which mirrors the East Stand across the pitch. These lower to just two tiers behind the goals, and the Tigers fans occupy a small section to my right.

Up above them is a large screen, one of two in the ground, and as part of the pre-match hype, it is showing a stirring selection of Manchester City goals, past and present, but mainly dwelling on the Colin Bell era. Blaring musical accompaniment for the goal montage is provided by an Oasis cover of David Bowie's *Heroes*.

It makes me realise that until Man City win something, or at least qualify for the Champions League, they will always be stuck in the past, rather like Hull City were until we broke into the Premiership. Chilton and Wagstaff don't seem like such super heroes any more, as they never actually took us into the top division.

All in all, it is an excellent ground, except for two minor niggles. The first of these is the name: The City of Manchester Stadium. It's a bit unimaginative and far too long, hence the developing tendency to refer to it as Eastlands, after the district, although, judging by the barren estate that I just walked through, 'Wastelands' might be more appropriate.

The second niggle is the black goal nets. These are completely invisible from a distance and it is hard to tell if the ball has hit the back of the net, as there is no discernible ripple. This is a worrying backward step in goal net technology, something that seems to be creeping in from the continent, along with other dangers like diving and Alice bands.

It is no coincidence that the goals being scored today are far more spectacular thanks to stanchion-free white nets. I watched an old video recently of 101 great goals from the 70's and 80's and it was amazing how often the ball bounced back out of the goal because it hit the stanchion, or because the net was too taut, thus, ruling them out as 'goal of the season' contenders. Upton Park and Loftus Road spring to mind here.

Otherwise, like I said, a brilliant stadium.

The Match – 8 out of 10 (from a neutral point of view)

The first fifteen minutes are quite open, and there is little indication of the impending massacre. The next fifteen minutes are quite open too, but only at one end.

It all begins to go wrong when Richard Dunne is allowed to carry the ball out of defence, and our half-hearted challenges make him look like an Olympic sprinter. He feeds Robinho, who audaciously chips a pass over McShane, finding Ireland. He hits the by-line before pulling back for the unmarked Caceido to rifle into the roof of the net. It's a brilliantly worked goal, and it could have won 'goal of the month' if it wasn't for the black nets.

It is too painful to provide such detail for the next three goals, but suffice to say, we contribute generously to our own downfall. A series of misdirected headers between Zayatte and Ashbee help to set up number two. Boeteng appears to be weighed down by the after effects of an excessive Christmas Day for the third, when he is easily robbed by Ireland, who sets up Robinho for a top Brazilian finish.

'Ireland is Superman,' sing the home fans. So Boeteng must be Lois Lane. She always used to fall over when being chased.

Sean Wright-Phillips is left unmarked to set up the fourth, in acres of space out on the right touchline. McShane probably mistook him for a ball boy.

At this stage, I look to the heavens for some kind of divine sign that things may get better, but it is a cloudless day, and all that I can see is an expanse of sky blue. Not the sign that I was looking for, and there seems little chance of a glorious amber sunset.

Half-time arrives, mercifully, and I am reminded of what it used to feel like to be a Hull City fan, not so many years ago: travelling great distances, spending pots of cash, sacrificing Saturdays; all in the name of humiliation.

What makes it worse today, is that I'm stuck in the middle of the Man City fans, who are all convinced that this performance heralds the dawn of a new era. Several of them are texting or phoning friends, explaining how the Robinho factor has turned them into Brazil. Even Richard Dunne has bombed forward like a young spring-heeled Socrates. I yearn to turn round and put them straight. Don't they realise that even Leeds would have looked good against us this afternoon!

Phil Brown is thinking the same thing. He feels our humiliation. He directs his forlorn players and staff across to the City faithful, where he applauds the loyal support, before sitting them down on the turf for a good old-fashioned bollocking. I should think so too. If they insist on playing like a pub side, then they need to accept the full experience with all the trimmings. If we had been playing at home, he could have got them to carry in the nets and posts after the game.

Had we not been 4-0 down, I might have found the second half good value for money. We enjoy a large share of the possession, and create some decent opportunities. The fire is back in the bellies, but it has completely gone from Man City's, and it is clear that they are already saving their legs for the fixture with Blackburn in two days time.

We eventually force a deserved goal, when Fagan, our energetic sub, scrambles in a rebound from Cousin's strike. This just serves to stoke up Man City, and they immediately summon up a fifth, just to remind us that they are not really trying any more. This time, Stephen Ireland is the unmarked recipient of Robinho's pull back.

The only other incidents of note after this are a couple of comedy moments from Paul McShane. The first comes when he just fails to reach an over-hit pass down the right wing, which runs out for a goal kick. He follows through into a giant microphone and kicks it in frustration, tangling his foot up in the wire in the process, to the great amusement of the home crowd. It takes him a good minute to work himself free.

But, the McShane Show has not finished yet. As if he hasn't suffered enough with the scoreline, the half time bollocking and the lost fight with the microphone, he manages to slip and fall flat on his back during another failed raid. Instead of just getting up normally, he rolls back onto his shoulders, feet in the air, and attempts an outrageous gymnastic spring back to his feet. This fails miserably, achieving only 45 degrees instead of the required 90, and he falls back to earth again. The over indulged fans in the south stand lap it up.

I'm seriously tempted to leave early, against my code of football conduct, but I see it out to the bitter end; bitter being the operative word.

Character – 5 out of 10

This is not a place to come if you are looking for a bit of character, as it is a very new development, but it is good to see distinctive features in and around the stadium. The outer spiral walkways are definitely unique, and the inside is instantly distinguishable from other stadia. The sky blue colour scheme is fairly rare, and it can't be confused with Coventry, as the Ricoh Arena is very different in design.

The nearest I come to a bit of nostalgia is the regular reminders of their happy days of the 1970's. Colin Bell and friends haunt the place like ghosts of the past, and the sooner they call in an exorcist, the better.

Paul Collingwood

Summary

I really appreciated Phil Brown's half time sentiments. He just wanted to apologise to the fans for wasting our Boxing Day. It was not an attempt to humiliate the players.

He knew only too well that I had spent £28 on the ticket, £40 on petrol, £5.50 on the M6 Toll, £3 on a programme, £3 on a cheeseburger and £1.50 on a bag of Revels for the journey. Grand total - £81.

Still, it's the tenth away game of our debut Premiership season, and it is the first time I have come away without a feeling of immense pride.

Matchday Experience Total – 39 out of 50

GOODISON PARK

Saturday 10th January 2009 – 3pm

Everton 2-0 Hull City

Accessibility 6 out of 10

To be honest, I'm getting a bit fed up with the M6 route to Lancashire. This is our fifth fixture in this neck of the woods, and we still have the Wigan and Bolton visits to enjoy. I must be financing the M6 toll road almost single-handed.

The usual anxiety about locating the stadium has been dispelled by my new satellite navigation system, although I needn't have worried; it is extremely well signposted from junction 26 onwards.

Having tapped in the Goodison postcode, I may well be guided to the centre circle of the pitch, but I will be on the look out for parking opportunities well before then. No such facilities present themselves, though, and I am drawn closer and closer to the ground. Eventually, I'm informed that I have reached my destination, and a sign is spotted offering matchday parking for £10. It's a bit steep, but doorstep parking obviously comes at a price. The alternative is to drive around aimlessly for the next half an hour, which would seriously wind up the Sat Nav, so I bite the bullet and open the wallet. Any thoughts of a quick getaway after the game are immediately quashed, as the money grabbing attendants gain maximum returns by arranging the cars like sardines in a tin. I end up right in the middle.

Facilities – 7 out of 10

Just across the road is the main car park for players and officials. I mosey over and immediately spot the McAllister Clan loitering around in the biting wind. Already, they appear to have come across another friend from Hull, but as I look more closely, I realise that they have accosted the City chairman, Paul Duffen. They set up a quick photo, as do a few other early arrivals, before Mr. Duffen finally breaks free and escapes into the ground.

Martin and Joe hang around for a while, autograph hunting, so Hugh and I set off on an outer tour of the stadium. This takes us first down Goodison Road, which runs at an inconvenient angle down the back of the main stand; an angle which effectively slices off the near corner, turning it's aerial view into an irregular elongated pentagon instead of a rectangle. A number of take-away eating establishments face the stand across the narrow street, and a variety of stalls have set themselves up for the day, selling scarves, badges, flags and the like.

At the far end, on the corner with the oddly named 'Gwladys Street,' we find the church of St. Luke the Evangelist. A plaque on the wall declares, 'Everton F.C. is the only club in the Football League to have built its ground in the back garden of a church.' Roughly translated, this means that, it is the only church within the grounds of a football club and they are lucky not to have been demolished to make way for more seats.

We boldly venture through the doors, thinking that we are entering the church, but it feels more like we have entered a spaghetti western. We have inadvertently walked into the church hall, and it is full of Everton fans, enjoying some kind of private pre-match function. A hush descends; eyes narrow, and the two strangers in town reverse slowly out through the saloon doors.

Little else of interest is discovered on the rest of the circuit, except for several intimidating policeman in Bullens Road, who all seem to have been issued with very long truncheon-type implements – ideal for civilians who contain excessive amounts of shit, and need it beating out of them.

The icy wind is really starting to bite, and nothing more can be gained from our tour, except maybe influenza. I'll bet Geovanni is sitting in the dressing room, wondering how it ever came to this.

Back in the car park, I treat myself to a burger, and my hands nearly freeze off. I may have to rethink my policy of not bringing gloves to football this winter, if only to assist with burger eating.

As soon as the gates open, we're in. It's not a lot warmer on the inside, but at least it's sheltered, and there is no wind-chill. Michele and Hugh make a beeline for the food stand for their regulation pies. They come back with two meat and potato offerings, which keep us occupied for a while with a little game of, 'spot the meat.'

My hunger has already been satisfied, so I just get a coffee. I'm asked if I want black or white. I want white. I'm given black, as you have to put your own milk in anyway. Strange.

I then get a text from Gary. We regularly used to brave the Boothferry terraces together, but now he is a resident of Liverpool. He has come to the game with Bob, a wheelchair bound friend, and they have just settled themselves in to the disabled section, right in front of the City fans at pitch side. I make my way down and Gary opens a small gate allowing me onto the gravel at the side of the pitch, right next to the City players who are busy warming up.

It's the first time I've been able to inspect the disabled facilities. A long row of numbered berths stretch along the touchline, each containing a padded pull-down seat and space for a wheelchair. If you like the ground level view, then they are great seats, but if you like being hit in the face by a ball and getting soaking wet, then they're not so good. Bob is a Tranmere Rovers fan, so he is actually here as Gary's guest, rather than the other way round.

For some reason, Bob is not too keen to reminisce about Hull City's last two meetings with Tranmere, four years ago, which produced a 9-2 aggregate in our favour. As we chat, Paul Duffen appears, and proceeds to shake hands with everyone. I think he's following me around.

The toffee girls come next. They are dressed in old-fashioned attire, and derive great pleasure from dipping their hands into a dainty basket, and pelting toffees at the crowd. Patronisingly, they toss one onto Bob's lap, but it slides off onto the floor. He's not too keen, so I eat it. It's a mint humbug, which by my reckoning, is no more a toffee than a pineapple chunk.

I'm quite enjoying my pitch-side freedom, wondering around with the stewards. A feeling of self-importance comes over me, but I stop short of testing out the playing surface, due in part to an amusing 'keep off the grass' sign, which reads: 'Grass grows by the inch, but is ruined by the foot.'

The Stadium – 6 out of 10

The Bullens Road Stand would surely have constituted a fire hazard if smoking were still allowed in grounds. It's the first time I have ever taken my place and found myself standing on wood, and a fair amount of discarded paper has found its way into the cracks between beams, waiting for a dropped cigarette. Just for good measure, the seats are wooden too.

I'm right at the back of the lower tier, but the upper tier dips to quite a low level ahead of us, so any high balls will be disappearing from view. You certainly wouldn't want to watch a Stoke match here.

Only the bottom tier is visible of the main stand opposite, and a stroll down to the front is required to see it in all its splendour. Granted, it's past its sell-by date, but they don't make 'em like that any more. The second tier suffers from traditional view-restricting girders, and I wouldn't fancy sitting at the top of the precariously steep third tier.

In the far right corner sits St. Luke's church, but the aesthetic qualities of this unique feature have been overridden by the 21st century desire to watch instant replays, so a giant screen has been erected in front of it. Another screen takes up space diagonally opposite, and this might be useful to me, as one of those irritating girders is right in my line of vision with the opposite goalmouth.

The Match – 4 out of 10

This drab game is easily summarised. Everton have three goal attempts in the first half and score twice. City don't have any. Neither keeper has to make a save in the second half.

There you are. Seriously, that is all that happened. It's hard to believe that two sides can play out 94 minutes with so few attempts to achieve the object of the game. Even the two goals that *were* scored should never have been allowed. Fellaini is a mile offside for the first (fact – not opinion) and the award of the free-kick that led to the second was soft, to say the least. Arteta's ability to strike a dead ball with venom was the one moment of class in the whole game, although questions will be asked about the manliness of our wall and positioning of our keeper, when a hit and hope thirty yarder can find the net so easily.

In such games, one has to look at the bigger picture for a bit of entertainment. The crowd usually helps, with witty songs to bait the opposition. My favourite today is one that focuses on the criminal reputation of the Merseyside city.

'You only sing when you're thieving.'

This reminds me of the extortionate £10 car park, and I start to worry about the well-being of my vehicle. With such fees, I feel like

I've been robbed once already, and I just pray that it won't be propped up on four piles of bricks when I return.

Marouane Fellaini is an interesting character. I spend a lot of time observing his contribution to the game, and I really can't make up my mind if he is a class act or a pile of shit. He certainly doesn't look like a professional footballer, at six foot five inches (six foot eight with the afro hair) and he ambles around as if he owns the place. He never seems to break into a sprint, but he manages to commit plenty of fouls. Eventually, he gets booked for a high challenge, and very nearly gets sent off for arguing about it. David Moyes substitutes him before this happens. I suppose he'll be worth the trouble if he scores a few vital goals, like he did today, but the question still remains: asset or liability?

Throughout the game, we are subjected to regular announcements about possible traffic congestion in the city centre after the game. Apparently, a certain section of the city will be closed from 7 o'clock, while they celebrate the end of their year as European City of Culture. Now, there's a joke. I'm not sure what the criteria are for this prestigious accolade, but the application process can't be very stringent. The last British city to receive the honour was Glasgow in 1990. Hull must be in with a shout then.

Anyway, back on the pitch, City belatedly throw on some extra forwards in the final minutes and muster a couple of strikes at goal, both off target. I slip out of the ground with two minutes of stoppage time remaining. We won't score even if two hours are added. Any hopes of beating the traffic are thwarted when I get to the car park and find that the gates are still shut. At least it was secure. I don't get moving for another half an hour.

Character – 9 out of 10

This is one of the oldest grounds in the football league and it still contains many traditional features. The wooden Bullens Road Stand was completed in 1926, and it really shows it. I love the design of the Main Stand, which is relatively new (1971) as it reminds me of how football grounds used to look when I was an impressionable child.

Undoubtedly, though, the best feature is St. Luke's Church, hiding away in the corner. I wonder if there was an outcry from fans when the big screen went up. It must surely have been a contentious decision, however much they need to show replays. Would Fulham ever put a screen in front of the cottage? I doubt it.

Summary

It has been another wasted day, and the standard of football being served up by the Tigers is massively disappointing, considering how we were fearlessly attacking sides earlier in the season. We gained 20 points from our first 9 games, but we've only taken seven from the next twelve. Everton were playing with no strikers today due to injuries, and Tim Cahill was pushed forward as the lone front man. If we had really gone for it, they were there for the taking.

Matchday Experience Total – 32 out of 50

UPTON PARK

Wednesday 28th January 2009 – 8pm

West Ham United 2-0 Hull City

Paul Collingwood

Accessibility – 6 out of 10

I love the London Underground. I'm not a daily commuter, obviously, otherwise I would hate it, but it is an extremely efficient mode of transport when in good working order. I never cease to be amazed whenever I turn up on a platform to discover that the next train is only two or three minutes away.

Tonight, the District Line is running smoothly, and there are plenty of seats, but they gradually fill with claret and blue passengers as we get nearer to Upton Park Station. The atmosphere is peaceful; pretty much like any other Wednesday night on the tube.

But the calm is soon shattered after a stop at Tower Hill, when a raucous cockney voice begins to reverberate around the carriage. A stocky shaven-headed Hammers fan, with an interesting assortment of earrings (several in the nose) is striking up one-way conversations with anyone who is careless enough to catch his eye. Then he spots my bright amber scarf.

It is only 6:30, but he has clearly already had a skinful, and he staggers down the carriage to take the empty seat by my side. Brilliant!

A quick glance at the topological map above the window tells me that I may be stuck with my new friend for another seven stops. Fortunately, he is full of admiration for the way Hull City have stormed the Premiership this season, and we manage to hold a half intelligent conversation (my half being the intelligent half).

He then gets disturbingly excited when the subject of Millwall fans trashing the KC Stadium comes up. This puts me on my guard again, and I'm forced to decline his kind invitation to go drinking with him in the *Queens*. I explain that I have to meet my brother in the *Mango Leaf*, which should get me off the hook, but he's never heard of it, and he suspects that I've made it up.

At Upton Park Station, we shake hands, and head off in different directions, agreeing that we'll probably bump into each other again next season. Not if I can help it.

At this point, I need to fast forward to the journey home, which is not quite so straightforward. All 40,000 fans, it seems, head for the tube station at the same time, but to prevent congestion at the main entrance, everyone is initially directed down a side street; a very long side street. Down at the end, we are asked to head up back towards the station, on the pavement, which is cordoned off by railings and scores of policemen, so you can't hop over and jump the queue.

It's incredibly frustrating to be walking in the wrong direction, and it's even more frustrating when we reach the bottleneck at the bottom, where no one moves for twenty minutes. It is gone ten o'clock and I begin to wonder if I'm going to get home tonight.

Eventually, the line creeps forward, and we get on a packed train. There is just one more low point to negotiate, though, when I decide to change at Monument. A network of underground tunnels, stairs and escalators should connect me to Bank, but they are closed for repairs, so I have to come up to street level and follow signs through the drizzle to make the connection. It is a surreal moment, wandering through the streets of London at 11 o'clock at night, tired, cold and hungry. I hate the London Underground.

Facilities – 6 out of 10

The 'Nutter on the Tube,' (Graham, to his friends), swears blind that the *Mango Leaf* does not exist, so I ring Peter to double check. He is already in there, sampling the beer, but I strongly insist that he nips back outside to read the pub sign. The name is confirmed, and a detailed description of the frontage is provided: old and ornate, apparently.

When I finally walk through the doors, I am surprised by the bright, modern interior with laminated floors and high stools. It extends back quite a long way to accommodate an eating area with a Chinese buffet. I resist the oriental aroma and head for the bar, where I meet Peter and two of his friends, Mike and Colin. The latter is a West Ham fan that Peter knows from his son's junior football team.

Colin reckons that I've had a lucky escape by avoiding *the Queens*. My scarf may not have been welcome, although it could have been useful for stringing me up.

Tonight's match is being covered by Sky, and a large TV screen on the wall is displaying the handsome faces of Jamie Rednapp and Dean Windass as they carry out their punditry duties. Mike refers to them as 'Beauty and the Beast,' but that's a bit harsh. Jamie isn't that ugly.

A couple of swift beers later, we are ready to move, but I think we are cutting it a bit too fine. Colin assures me that we will make it in good time for kick off, but he hasn't accounted for the pile up at the away end, where meticulous body searches are being conducted. There are five turnstiles in operation, which should be enough, but the slow frisking process causes us to miss kick off.

Despite this, the hot dog stand is still my first port of call, as I'm bloody starving. It's probably the best time to eat, as there are no queues. Everyone else is either in their seats or still outside being fondled. I discover later, at half time, that the long narrow corridor is not roomy enough for a following such as ours, which always takes up its full ticket allocation.

The Stadium – 8 out of 10

It is not possible to fairly assess the outside of Upton Park, as it is very dark and rather late when we pitch up. The route to the away end leads us down a side street and through a bus station, and before we know it, the Centenary Stand is towering over us.

The view from our seats makes up for the missed external observations. The scale of the place pleasantly surprises me, although visual clarity is slightly impaired by the fine misty drizzle that has been falling all day. The meaty two-tiered West Stand would befit any Premier League ground. Networks of staircases are visible at the extremities, as they wind their way up into the heavens, or down into the bowels, depending on your point of view. Two big screens are in operation: one just to our left, and another diagonally opposite. This seems to be the norm at most Premiership grounds now.

The East Stand, to our left, is the only stand that doesn't measure up. It's not bad really, but the majestic West Stand must be giving it an inferiority complex.

Our seats are just five rows from the front, close to the corner flag, not that anyone is bothering to sit down. The steady drizzle drifts into our faces on the chill January breeze, and the entire City section opts to stand throughout.

I am yearning for some springtime weather, when I can shed the ski jacket, and show off the expensive short-sleeved flint-coloured away top that I got for Christmas.

The Match – 6 out of 10

We haven't missed much while queuing for the hot dog. City look quite comfortable early on, and a false optimism begins to build. The Hammers soon get into gear though, courtesy of some hesitant defending from Zayatte, (another person who can't wait for the first blossoms of spring).

The chances begin to flow. Di Michele comes closest, rattling the post with a beautifully executed curling effort from outside the box. Then, we witness a laughable dive in the area by Carlton Cole, followed by an even more laughable decision from the referee. He is clearly a referee of the 'homer' variety, and his judgement is clouded by strong appeals from the biased home support, who know in their heart of hearts that it was a dive. I can't blame them for trying. We would have done the same if the boot was on the other foot, although Carlton Cole's boots might be too big for Geovanni.

However, the ref caves in and awards it, and the stadium is filled with rousing cheers and a fair amount of laughter from shocked Eastenders, who can't believe their luck.

Matt Duke soon wipes the smiles off their faces, though, by brilliantly saving Mark Noble's accurate spot kick, and suddenly it is our turn to laugh and cheer. Maybe… just maybe… this is going to be our night.

Or maybe not. Duke's fortunes take a turn for the worse when he deflects a low cross from Cole straight onto the on-rushing knee of Di Michele. 1-0, and further chances follow, thick and fast, but our luck somehow holds.

This game is starting to follow a similar pattern to the one at Everton, in that we don't look like scoring before midnight. (A visit to their penalty box would be nice). Unlike Everton, the Hammers look dangerous, and I'm worried that they could run in three or four.

During the interval, Peter and I agree that a couple of half time substitutions are necessary. Bullard and Mendy are the preferred options.

We can't believe it when City trot out for the second half with no changes in personnel. The Hammers go 2-0 up with their first serious attack. Brown then brings on Bullard. A phrase comes to mind, which includes the words: stable, door, shutting, horse and bolted.

I'm sure Jimmy is delighted to be making his debut in such hopeless circumstances, but give the man credit, he immediately starts to run the midfield, and very nearly pulls a goal back with a swerving 25 yard strike. Rob Green thwarts him by springing to his right for his only save of the game. (Nice work if you can get it).

We press more and more, but West Ham are content to hit us on the counter, and we are thankful to Matt Duke (making his Premiership debut) for keeping the scoreline respectable. Ashbee provides Bullard with a hospital pass late on, and the ensuing crunching tackle sees him limping for the rest of the game, which soon fizzles out. We all troop off, thoroughly depressed, having endured the third inept away performance in a row. I'm not sure why we suddenly look so beatable, when we were so inspired before Christmas.

Character – 7 out of 10

West Ham is a club with a very proud tradition, which loosely means: they used to be good, but not any more. Gianfranco Zola and Steve Clarke are trying to restore the free flowing brand of football that their crowd has come to expect, and on tonight's display, they are making a good fist of it. My new friend from the tube seemed quite optimistic about the present regime, and he was content to accept attacking football in mid table rather than emulate the multi-rich big four by spending your way to success.

Back in 1966, the Hammers famously supplied the backbone of England's World Cup squad, with home grown talent, and there has been a steady flow of talent coming through the ranks ever since.

The stadium is another old ground trapped in residential London, so they have done very well to redevelop it to its present size. The hold up at the turnstiles certainly felt like a trip back in time, and the facilities underneath the Centenary Stand were a bit Spartan, but in general, it is a decent ground.

Summary

Tonight was a forgettable experience. It was cold and wet, we were poor, and I didn't get home until after midnight. I'm very busy at work this week, and I really didn't want to be here. Jimmy Bullard probably feels the same way. His injury turns out to be more serious than it looked. He will miss the rest of the season. That's money well spent: five million pounds for 38 minutes.

It would have been totally different had we won, though. All of my cares would have disappeared. That's what football can do for you: build you up or drag you down, and tonight, I'm as low as you can go.

Matchday Experience Total – 33 out of 50

STAMFORD BRIDGE

Saturday 7th February 2009 – 3pm

Chelsea 0-0 Hull City

Paul Collingwood

Accessibility – 5 out of 10

Originally, I was going to attend today's game with my brother, Peter, so he was naturally delighted when his son qualified for a half time penalty shoot out at the League Two game between Brentford and Chester, on the same day. Being the dutiful parent, he's off to Griffin Park, but I know where he would rather be.

I have persuaded my brother-in-law, Brian, to come along instead. Brian supports Manchester United; so fittingly, he will want the Tigers to win by a huge margin. We hope to meet up with his brother and sister-in-law, Kevin and Maura, in a members only pub, *The Black Bull*, near to the ground. They are both Chelsea fanatics, and season ticket holders at the Bridge, so the pre-match deliberations will have a three way split of allegiance.

Brian turns up in a bright amber raincoat, which is a highly encouraging start. I'm glad to see that he is taking his responsibilities as Peter's last minute replacement so seriously. He seems full of enthusiasm and he's really up for it, although I haven't told him the price of the ticket yet, (£47). I'll save that little bombshell until we reach the point of no return.

Quite why Abramovich, (a billionaire let's remember), needs to charge such exorbitant prices for ninety minutes of football is beyond me. But then, he's not a billionaire for nothing.

The journey is all planned. We will arrive at Hemel Station at midday, and the Black Bull by two. But, if there is one thing you can rely on in this country, it's the unreliability of our trains, especially after a week of unusually heavy snow, so the 12:08 train has been re-scheduled for 12:50. It eventually rolls in at 12:58. We then make a bad decision, by jumping off at Watford Junction in the hope of making a quick connection for West Brompton.

There are two little clues that should have encouraged us to stay put. Firstly, none of the other Chelsea fans get off, and secondly, lots more get on.

A frustratingly long wait at Watford, is followed by a slow train to Willesden, and two different tube lines to Fulham Broadway. Several texts to Maura and Kevin inform them of our predicament, but I blame the trains instead of my incompetence. If we had just stayed on the first Euston train, we would have made it on time.

Instead, we shuffle off a crowded 2:40 arrival at Fulham Broadway and head straight for the ground. Shame, because I'm gasping for a drink.

Facilities – 9 out of 10

If there is one ground you want to arrive early at, it's Stamford Bridge. There are stacks of pubs and restaurants in close proximity, not to mention a number of bars, grills and hotels, which form part of the stadium site. In the days of Ken Bates (sorry, didn't mean to swear), it was known as the Chelsea Village, but now it is just referred to as the Stamford Bridge Complex. Not quite as catchy.

On the mad dash to the City end, we pass between the Millennium Hotel and Frankie's Bar & Grill, but we don't have time to go and sample whatever Frankie is grilling. Actually, it is highly unlikely that Frankie is there, as the Frankie in question is the celebrated jockey, Frankie Dettori, part owner in the joint, and I'm sure he's got better things to do on a Saturday afternoon than slave over a hot grill, waiting on half-cut football fans.

Programmes are sold from several evenly spaced stalls, each with a small blue and white umbrella erected overhead. The brollies are for decoration, I assume, as they would offer meagre protection against any serious shower of rain. I decide to stop and buy one as a souvenir, just in case our season goes tits up, and we don't visit here again. Current league form suggests that it's a distinct possibility.

Next stop is the turnstiles, where a feeble attempt at frisking is being undertaken by a squad of security guards, who don't seem very well qualified for the job. I'm apprehensive, because I have a number of bulky items inside my jacket, including: phone, keys, wallet, programme and a camera the size of a brick. One gentle pat of the pockets, and I'm ushered through. No one seems concerned about the brick.

I'm then faced with a second line of security, but instead of receiving a more thorough examination, I'm politely asked if I have already been searched. Everyone is saying that they have, even if they haven't. Yo really wouldn't want these guys working at Heathrow just before you board a flight to the Middle East.

We get through shortly before kick off, and I just have time to grab a hot dog and a Mars Bar, placing another £4 into the deep pockets of a certain Russian oil baron.

Stadium – 8 out of 10

Our late arrival means that I can't study the outside of the stadium too closely, but from what I can see, it looks quite striking. All of the extras that have been added on to the South Stand make it a busy place to be prior to kick off. Ken Bates certainly knew what he was doing when he commissioned this project, which makes a change from being an arsehole. Mind you, it did help to drag the club deep into financial ruin, prompting the Russian takeover. Bates is now applying his inverted form of the Midas touch to Leeds United. They are well suited.

Our seats are in the Shed End, unthinkable a few years ago, when it was the Chelsea nutter's stronghold. We are in the upper tier, near to the corner flag, and it provides us with an excellent panoramic view.

The East Stand to my right holds three tiers, while four can be defined in the West Stand. Two narrow middle bands obviously hold the corporate section, as they completely empty at half time – and I mean, completely. Not one soul remains. There must be some incredible prawn sandwiches on offer back inside, but if Abramovich has anything to do with it, they won' be free.

The stands behind the goals are smaller, and have only two tiers. As usual, two big screens are available to give us replays of anything non-contentious.

The Match – 7 out of 10

Suggs' lesser hit from 1997, *Blue Day*, is blaring out in the build up to kick off, and it continues for a few seconds after as well. I glance up from my programme to find that the match is already under way, with Chelsea kicking towards us.

We are under pressure from the start, but John Terry drops a hint that this could be an *Amber Day* rather than a *Blue Day* by spooning a simple chance over the bar from two yards. Matt Duke then pulls off a superb diving save to deny Ricardo Quaresma a debut goal.

We gradually work our way into the game, and create some good chances of our own, Kilbane's header against the post being the best. The closest Chelsea come after this is a blast from Lampard, which embeds itself in Zayatte's nuts. He takes a while to get to his feet, and a good ten minutes to fully straighten out.

Half time arrives, and it is goalless: a pleasing state of affairs. Brian and I go for a stroll along the crowded walkway under the stand. Heading west, I bump into the unmistakable Martin, in his distinctive furry tiger headgear. Not only does this 'hat' keep his ears warm, but it also gets him a few appearances on Match of the Day, and the occasional interview. He is happy to look ridiculous in return for such riches. We agree that City are unlucky not to lead, and a general air of optimism is wafting down the corridor.

Chelsea enjoy most of the possession in the second half, but City look dangerous on the counter attack. The best chances fall to the boys in amber and black, with Fagan just failing to execute a chip over the luminous orange Hilario, and Marney flashing a shot millimetres wide.

Scolari is under pressure, and he decides to throw on some subs from his multi-million pound bench. Drogba and Deco enter the fray.

'Huh, is that the best you've got?' thinks Phil Brown. 'Anything you can do, we can do better!'

He brings on Ryan France.

However, we are able to hold out comfortably, and only a timely interception from Terry prevents Fagan from advancing on goal for a winner. Still, it's a fantastic point, and who knows how vital it could be come the end of May.

Character – 6 out of 10

Back in the 1970's, the King's Road was the place to be. The Chelsea players were the trendiest in town with their long hair, wing collars and silly tie knots. The first FA Cup Final that I can remember featu

Chelsea against Leeds in 1970, but two players from slightly before that era are paraded before the crowd prior to kick off.

Bobby Tambling and Barry Bridges are guests of honour, having made their debuts exactly fifty years ago today. The programme devotes several pages to their past glories (300 goals between them) including a 1966 team photo with Osgood, Bonetti, Hollins, Harris and Venables.

The stadium has changed a fair bit since those days. The famous Shed has long gone, although the name remains. I remember that there always seemed to be acres of space at Stamford Bridge between the pitch and the stands, but it is all a lot more compact today. Space existed behind the goals too, rather like Wembley

Summary

Oh, the shame of failing to beat Hull City. It is all too much for Roman Abramovich to take and Scolari is sent packing, although he may need some help carrying the cases of cash that he's made over the last eight months.

Unfortunately, this means that all the headlines will be deflected from a fantastic Tigers team effort. This was more like the performances from earlier in the season, and if we keep this up, we'll be fine. A special word of mention here to Craig Fagan who worked his socks off as a lone striker, giving Terry and Alex a torrid time. Shame he couldn't score to put the icing on the cake.

Brian and I did finally meet up with Maura and Kevin after the game, but they were not in a good mood. They had plenty to say though, and I would love to record it for posterity, but after removing all of the expletives, it just leaves me with the words: Chelsea, Hull and Scolari.

Matchday Experience Total – 35 out of 50

CRAVEN COTTAGE

Wednesday 4th March 2009 – 8pm

Fulham 0-1 Hull City

Paul Collingwood

Accessibility 8 out of 10

After the Chelsea travel fiasco, I decide to hit the railway station as early as possible, and as luck would have it, a train is just two minutes away. The downside to this is the lost opportunity to buy a newspaper for the journey, but one of those free London rags (full of adverts) has been conveniently abandoned on my seat. It will have to do.

The sports pages focus solely on the London sides, which is fine, as we are playing Fulham, but the article on the Tigers clash tells me nothing that I don't already know. Apparently, Roy Hodgson has decided that they are not missing Jimmy Bullard. Well, why would you miss a player with only one leg?

I resort to the general knowledge crossword, but I'm really struggling until I come to 21 and 22 down. 'Guinea International defender, signed by Hull City from Young Boys of Berne.'

Suddenly, I'm in business, and I'm sure I would have finished it if the train had not already been edging into Euston.

The efficient London Underground takes me the rest of the way, and I arrive far too early at Putney Bridge Station. My specific destination is the *Eight Bells* pub, which is appropriate, as we plan to knock seven bells out of Fulham tonight.

The plan is to meet Malcolm and Steve here, as they have my ticket. Steve is a season ticket holder at Fulham, and as such, he was able to buy extra discount tickets for the Neutral Stand for just £5 each. Malcolm, poor chap, is a Luton fan. He is just coming along in search of some meaningful football.

Facilities – 7 out of 10

The Eight Bells is a friendly little establishment, in a horseshoe shape, with the bar in the middle. I scan both sides of the horseshoe, but unsurprisingly, as it's so early, there is no sign of Steve or Malcolm. A quick phone call informs me that they will be at least half an hour, so go for a stroll.

It is dusk, and I reckon that I may be able to get a really arty photo raven Cottage if I cross the bridge and walk down the opposite side of the Thames. The bright floodlights are clearly visible, peering over the top of the riverside trees, so I dodge the rush hour traffic on Putney Bridge, and cross to the south bank. The bend of the river makes the distance deceptive. No matter how far I walk, the floodlights don't appear to be getting any nearer. It takes about fifteen minutes before I concede defeat and abandon the exercise.

I'm gasping for a drink by the time I make it back to the pub, but I'm briefly stalled at the doors by Mike and Jeremy, a couple of southern based supporters (Surrey and Kent respectively). I regularly cross paths with them at away games.

The bar is well prepared for thirsty football fans, with five bar staff in operation, so I'm soon back outside in the cold still air. Jeremy was in Hull at the weekend for our 2-1 submission to Blackburn, so he is not too confident. Mike is more optimistic, but only if Brown selects the correct team. There were some strange decisions made on Saturday.

Malcolm and Steve soon arrive and I hand over the money for the ticket. Administration costs bump the price up to £7.50, but it still bears no comparison to the £47 Chelsea rip off. Stamford Bridge may only be just down the road, but in many respects, the two clubs are worlds apart.

Mike and Jeremy leave first for the ground. Steve, with his superior local knowledge, tries to shout after them, to let them know that they are heading in the wrong direction. They can't hear. It is the last that we see of them on the night.

We sup up and leave, in the correct direction, via an underpass, which takes us beneath Putney Bridge. Hordes of fans from both sides join us on the riverside walk through well-maintained public gardens. Steve assures me that this would be a picturesque route to the ground if only it wasn't pitch dark.

Finally, we reach the cottage at the northeast corner of the ground, and Steve heads off to his usual seat, leaving Malcolm and me to seek out food at the back of the Putney Stand. Actually, Malcolm leaves the food seeking to me, while he joins the unacceptably long queue for the inadequate toilet facilities.

Two pre-packaged 'Rollover' hot dogs are purchased, and we proceed to the stand to find out exactly what is meant by 'Neutral.'

Paul Collingwood

The Stadium – 6 out of 10

I'm peeved that this fixture is an evening kick off. It is very dark in the streets outside the entrance, and I can't get a decent photo of the 'cottage' or the back of the Johnny Haynes Stand, which is quite elaborate in design. The ornate brickwork runs the full length of the northern outlook, and it seems far too grand to be wasted on a football ground. It would be much more at home as part of a stately country manor.

It turns out that this is the oldest operational stand in the Football League, and it is now a Grade II listed building. They certainly don't make them like this any more.

By contrast, the concourse at the back of the eastern Putney Stand is open air, with a low fence acting as a rear boundary. It looks like it would be really easy to sneak in without paying, or out, if the game is crap.

Several signs direct the away fans towards the far end, while the neutrals (that's Malcolm and me) are invited to climb a rather temporary looking staircase at the near end. This structure is not made from your standard cast-iron or concrete, but a hollow rattling aluminium, or possibly tin. We can safely assume that the Putney Stand will not be lasting over a hundred years like its friend round the corner.

The inside of the ground is better than I expected. The listed stand to our right is the smallest of the four, and a distinctive old-fashioned gable protrudes from the centre of the roof, displaying the club crest.

My eyes might be deceiving me, but the Hammersmith End, way in the distance, appears to be accommodating six lovely little balconies, rather like those you might see overlooking the sea on a holiday hotel. There are three on each side, stacked vertically, with a number of fans leaning on the railing, admiring the view. Malcolm informs me that there are private boxes behind them, but I can't see them from my position. Likewise, a select few are lined up on the balcony of the 'cottage,' tucked away in the corner to my right. It seems that the club have used every available space to bump the capacity up to the 25,000 mark.

There is no sign of a scoreboard, or big screen or clock. Then I notice something up above our heads, attached to the under side of the roof, looking suspiciously like the back of a scoreboard. Not much use to us.

Oh, and one more annoying thing; black nets again. I'll just have to assume that the goal down at the far end has actually got a net, because it doesn't look like it from our vantage point. Ridiculous. Bring back white nets!

The Match – 7 out of 10

The first five minutes are spent polishing off our hot dogs. Nothing much happens in this time until Mendy earns a free kick in Geovanni territory. The little Brazilian thumps the ball towards us, and it appears goal bound before swerving wide at the last second.

Thereafter, it is all Fulham, and our defence has to be alert to keep it goalless, although Matt Duke is rarely made to sweat. The same cannot be said for the second half, though, as our keeper is forced to tip over an Andy Johnson drive in the first minute. Further efforts rapidly follow from Konchesky and Dempsey, but Duke is equal to the task.

It is all one way, and we are barely ten minutes into the half. Malcolm is worried for me. 'Can you hang on for another forty minutes?' he asks.

I have to admit that it looks unlikely.

Around us, the Neutral Stand doesn't appear to be too neutral. Tigers fans far outweigh the Fulham fans, and the tension can be felt. We badly need something from this game as we are now just three points off the drop zone. It is a risky policy, allowing opposing fans to mix so freely, especially when the stakes are so high. Unsurprisingly, this is the only stand of its kind in the football league, and they had to apply for a special licence to get permission.

The pressure eases and Fulham's attacks become more sporadic. In the final fifteen minutes we begin to venture into their half a little more frequently, and then Manucho's introduction seems to breathe new life into our lungs.

The ninetieth minute is reached, and the board is held aloft signifying three extra minutes. I have accepted a point at this stage, and I just pray that Fulham don't break our hearts with a late strike.

We have thrown too many points away recently by conceding at the death.

But for once, finally, gloriously, it is the Tigers who snatch the points, and they couldn't have left it much later. Garcia plunders forward and hooks an inviting cross into the Fulham box. Manucho accepts the invitation while the Fulham defence appear to be checking their diaries. He bangs it into the net (a black invisible one) so I can't tell initially if the ball has actually gone in, and I daren't celebrate until I'm absolutely sure. But, the players appear to be going bonkers as they mob Manucho, and the Neutral stand belatedly goes ballistic, showing its true colours – black and amber.

You can't beat a late winner in a vital game. One point suddenly turns into three, and only a true football fan can understand the associated adrenaline rush. But crushing lows can often follow the wonderful highs, and we still have half a minute to negotiate. Fulham immediately force a corner. I won't be able to cope if they score now. The corner is deflected towards goal before being turned wide. Another corner. Duke comes for it and punches clear. The whistle goes, and the adrenaline pumps again.

The electronic advertising panels around the edge of the pitch flick up the slogan for LG, Fulham's shirt sponsors.

'Life's Good,' it says.

Character – 10 out of 10

Everything about the Fulham ground exudes character: the location by the Thames, the antiquated North Stand, and of course, the cottage in the corner. There are similarities here with Everton's ground, which uniquely boasts a church in the corner, but at least Fulham have resisted the temptation to hide it behind a bloody great big screen.

The original Craven Cottage was actually a hunting lodge and it burnt down in 1888. It was sited approximately where the centre circle now is, so it's just as well someone torched it, or it would have got in the way of the football. The present cottage was built in 1903 at the same time as the North Stand, and both are now listed buildings.

Steve gives me further information about the Johnny Haynes Stand after the game. The spacing of seats has remained unchanged for the past one hundred years, so anyone taller than 5ft 8in does not fit. People of Peter Crouch proportions were a bit of a rarity in Edwardian times, and they were probably too busy travelling with the circus to go and watch Fulham.

Summary

The feeling of euphoria at the final whistle is up there with the Arsenal game. Even Malcolm went mental when the goal went in. He's not a neutral any more.

My phone is buzzing on the walk back to the tube with a host of calls and texts. Everyone feels the relief. It was all doom and gloom after the home defeat to Blackburn, but now we are five points clear of trouble and the next game is at home to Newcastle. We have arrested the slide.

There are big wins and there are massive wins. This one was in the massive category.

Matchday Experience Total – 38 out of 50

JJB STADIUM

Sunday 22nd March 2009 – 1.30pm

Wigan Athletic 1-0 Hull City

Accessibility – 8 out of 10

An all-powerful satellite television channel has decreed that this game should take place early on a Sunday afternoon. As usual, we all obediently comply with its demands, regardless of the domestic meltdown that ensues with the discovery that it now clashes with Mother's Day.

However, there are two advantages to be gained from the unfortunate switch. Firstly, there is very little traffic on the roads at 8 am on the Sabbath; and secondly, the game is over by mid afternoon, so I can make it home in time for a late tea.

Signposts for the JJB are regular and clear along the A49 into Wigan, but several other signs intrigue me, making the extravagant claim that the town has something worthwhile to offer to the casual tourist. Despite being twenty miles from the coast, an effort is made to direct everyone to the mythical 'Wigan Pier.' This has featured for many years in comedic jokes and one-liners, but has now been adopted as the name for a new leisure park, boasting: shops, restaurants, entertainment venues and a museum. The museum has already closed down though, so it may soon become as invisible as the original pier, which did apparently exist, but it was just an insignificant wooden jetty on the canal. It obviously got ideas above its station; a bit like Wigan Athletic.

Facilities – 8 out of 10

I'm directed in a loop to the far side of the ground, where three large car parks await. Five pounds is the predictable asking price, but I hold fire until I've called Dave, in case he is in a pub on the other side of town. It turns out that he's in a pub on the other side of the stadium, the *Red Robin*, which is part of the Robin Park complex.

I re-loop the loop and find a convenient parking spot right opposite the pub, for £5 less than they are asking on the other side. A large banner outside is suggesting that families might like to book their Mother's Day meals here. I go inside and meet up with Dave, Gary, Chris and Ledge. There are no mothers in sight.

A happy two hours are spent with my ex school mates. The omens are good. The last time we all met up at a City game was last season at Leicester. We won that one convincingly, and we are all beginning to feel positive vibes.

Eventually, we force ourselves to saunter across the retail park towards the JJB Stadium. We spy the scoreboard through a gap between stands, and are worried by some of the names that we see flashing across the screen: Folan, Hughes, Garcia… For a moment, we think that Phil Brown is sending out an experimental formation, then we realise that we are looking at a list of the substitutes.

Any thoughts we may have had about visiting the club shop are quickly scuppered when we see a placard advertising that it will open in two weeks time. How strange. I assume that the sale of club merchandise is not a new concept to millionaire Dave Whelan, club chairman and owner.

The food situation is more promising, and there is no shortage of outlets underneath the North Stand. The large hot dog that I purchase also looks promising until I realise that the sausage is half the length of the roll. Once the sausage is gone, I'm basically left chewing on a soggy tomato sauce sandwich.

The Stadium – 6 out of 10

On a good day, the JJB Stadium holds 25,000 fans, but they haven't had a good day yet. With a total town population of barely 80 000, it will rarely be full, and the high density of football teams in the Lancashire region offers little hope of recruitment for fresh followers.

The architecture of the ten-year-old stadium is very precise and symmetrical. Opposite sides of the ground mirror each other perfectly, and the four separate rectangular stands leave open-air gaps in the corners. Seats rise up to the same level on all sides in one tier.

Surprisingly, the colour scheme is blue and red, which I can't quite understand. Wigan play in blue and white, and the JJB logo is blue and green. Gary reminds me that their kit has contained touches of red over the years, and that they had a red away strip until recently.

Some amusement comes from a banner laid out across the Sout' Stand seats. 'Local team, World Stars,' it reads. Someone needs to po' out to the Wigan fans that just because a player is foreign, it doesn't make him a world star. Despite the banner, and a smattering of early arrivals, I can still just make out the large white JJB lettering on the seats. I then realise that my own seat is white, and I calculate that I must be sitting in the middle of a large letter J. This might have to be ripped out next season when Dave Whelan re-names the ground after himself. It will become the DW Stadium.

Let's hope that this idea does not catch on with other egotistic chairmen who wish to further promote their own profiles. It could get very misleading in some cases. Phil Gartside's Bolton ground could be confused with PG Tips, and the BK Stadium at Everton might be linked with Burger King. Additionally, Villa could play at Randy Park, Derby at Pearson Park and Leeds at Pillock Park.

The Match – 5 out of 10

Both sides march purposefully out of the tunnel to the tune from Pirates of the Caribbean. I'm not sure of the relevance of the chosen music, but hopefully it signifies that Wigan will be 'all at sea.'

The game commences, with the Tigers kicking away from their loyal following, and a pattern of play soon develops: Wigan attack, and City defend. We survive until half time, just about, but if this is our master plan for Premiership survival, I'm not very impressed, and it's not very entertaining either. Wigan are a distinctly average side, but we haven't had one decent effort on goal.

Our half time analysis beneath the stand fails to sow any seeds of hope for the second half. Dave has developed a new catchphrase in recent weeks, and he has already repeated it several times today:

'I'd take a point.'

I have to agree. Judging by the first half performance, it is the best that we can hope for. However, football is a game of two halves, and they can often be totally different.

The early signs are good after the restart, and we are unfortunate not to take the lead when Manucho's header is brilliantly tipped over by Kirkland. But that is the last time that the former Liverpool keeper is forced to display his England credentials. Wigan resume control, though they don't look as dangerous as in the first half.

With ten minutes remaining, Wigan hit the post.

'I'd take a point,' Dave whispers.

But we are not going to get it. Three minutes later, a long throw is sent into the City box. Duke comes for the punch and half clears it, but Marney cannot deal with the other half of the clearance. Ben Watson nicks it off him and loops the ball over the stranded Duke, forcing the Wigan fans to come to life. We offer little in the way of goalscoring retaliation, and there is no suggestion that we can reclaim the point that Dave so desperately craves.

Character – 3 out of 10

Wigan were a non-league team just 21 years ago, so there is no tradition in terms of league football. They moved out of Springfield Park in 1999, and I do have a painful memory of an FA Cup fifth round visit in 1987 when we were turned over, 3-0.

The new stadium is too perfectly designed to show character, it doesn't have any interesting distinctive features, and it was half empty, so I'm being generous by giving it 3 out of 10.

Summary

This was another wasted day. We only had one serious attempt on goal, and we could have lost by more. Injuries forced us to reorganise the defence twice, but this cannot be used as a valid excuse. It keeps us in 13th spot, which sounds good, but we are only four points above the drop.

As we leave the ground, I receive a text from my depressed cousin, Hugh. He is planning to jump off Wigan Pier.

Matchday Experience Total – 30 out of 50

THE RIVERSIDE STADIUM

Saturday 11th April 2009 – 3pm

Middlesbrough 3-1 Hull City

Paul Collingwood

Accessibility – 7 out of 10

Annual 'crap town' surveys often like to place Hull and Middlesbrough at the top of the chart, which could explain why Britain's motorway network has chosen to steer well clear of the two much-maligned cities. Planning a direct route between two, is well nigh impossible, unless you happen to be the proverbial crow.

Martin's chosen route takes us initially to the outskirts of York, before we straighten up and follow the A19 via Thirsk. This is possibly more scenic than branching out to the A1, and it is slightly more direct, but is it any quicker?

Travelling on our nation's lesser 'A' roads can be an infuriating experience for frustrated rally drivers such as Martin. Our progress is stalled by a steady supply of buses, camper vans, tractors and pensioners, united in the common cause of cutting speed limits in half.

By the time we reach a McDonalds, on the northern fringes of the York ring road, a unanimous decision has been made to pull in for a late breakfast, or brunch, as our American friends insist on calling it. I'm indifferent to the brunch idea, until Martin produces a gold mine of vouchers from his pocket, entitling us to a range of freebies, courtesy of the recent Monopoly promotion. I end up with a random selection of side orders, rarely thrown together as part of the same meal, but it's free!

This sets us up nicely for the second half of the journey, with Joe and Martin even helping themselves to free top-ups to their free drinks, which I'm sure you're not meant to do.

By 12:30 we are approaching the outer limits of Middlesbrough, and judging by our first impression, it fully warrants its standing as Britain's crappest town. It can't be too far from securing the top spot in Europe either. Factories, chimneys and derelict warehouses dominate the skyline, and I can see why the locals are known affectionately as 'smoggies.'

The Riverside Stadium is clearly sign-posted, but we are in no desperate hurry to arrive, as Hugh remembers from his previous visit that it is sited in the middle of a bleak industrial park (although this could describe just about any building in Middlesbrough). We turn off the A19 and follow signs for the university, jumping to the conclusion that wherever you find students, you'll find pubs.

Facilities – 7 out of 10

'Pub ahoy!'

Like a vigilant seafarer scanning the horizon from the crow's nest, Michele spots the *White Rose* long before the rest of the crew. Our Hull City shirts receive a warm welcome at the bar, and it is most encouraging to learn that every Boro fan in residence, is predicting a Tigers victory. Pessimism and depression are in the blood round here, which is understandable when you take in the surroundings.

Michele is relying increasingly on superstition to secure our premiership survival, so it is vital that she orders a dry white wine. Apparently, we have never lost whenever she has relied on the magical powers of this drink before a game. She then suggests that the *White Rose* pub name could also be a good omen, until we remind her that Middlesbrough is in Yorkshire too.

We hang around long enough to catch the first half of Liverpool's clash with Blackburn, and leave the pub happy, as Torres puts them 2 up against one of our relegation rivals.

On the way to the ground, Michele starts banging on about how she has spotted five black and amber taxis, and how this obviously means that we will score five goals. I don't have the heart to tell her that I've spotted ten red ones.

A parking space is found on Dockside Road, next to the railway line, but there is a long walk to the stadium, and it's not a scenic one. The region appears to be rich in scrap heaps, breaker's yards and household waste depots, but the highlight of the stroll is the crossing over a murky drainage channel, which provides a putrid smell befitting of the whole area.

By the time we reach the turnstiles, I'm desperate to visit the urinals, so I go straight through, while the McAllisters seek out the club shop. Hugh is close to completing his collection of Premiership mugs but Joe has abandoned his quest for cushions. Worryingly though, for a 2 year old, this fetish has been replaced by a compulsion to collect cude toy mascots. He arranges these along the headboard of his bed to I him company through the long winter nights. What he really needs is a girlfriend.

Today's cuddly collectable is a red lion, as depicted on the Middlesbrough badge, but Joe is outraged to learn that it is called Roary. There is only one Roary, and he's a tiger!

Meanwhile, inside the ground, my hunger has returned. The delights of our daylight robbery raid on McDonalds have worn off, and I'm now in a queue for a £2 minced beef pie. The selection at the food outlet is disappointing: pie, beer or chocolate, basically.

The Stadium – 7 out of 10

The toilet situation reduces the opportunity to survey the outside of the ground. From most angles, it is big, grey and dull, but from the western aspect there are plenty of red splashes and the club name is prevalent. The bladder is contained just about long enough to allow a sprint across the car park for a photo of the main entrance.

Inside, it reminds me a little bit of Pride Park in size and shape, apart from the red seats. From my viewpoint, behind the goal, I can see a large two-tiered stand to my left, while the rest of the ground makes do with one large tier.

There is no space for big screens, but a couple of electronic scoreboards are bracketed to the undersides of the roof, above the goals. The starting line-ups are running across these, and it soon becomes apparent that Marlon King has been given a start for Middlesbrough, and George Boateng has returned for City, albeit on the bench. Both selections should add a little extra spice to proceedings.

Four thousand City fans are out in force, filling the south stand and making a lot of noise. There are 32,000 fans inside the stadium altogether, but only a small group in the near corner of the East Stand seem willing to compete with the Tigers contingent. They must be losing the faith.

The Match – 7 out of 10

'e could really do with an early goal to settle the nerves, but instead, gift one to Middlesbrough. Ashbee and Zayatte conspire to lose the ball; it breaks to King; he forces Duke into a save, but Tuncay follows up to send the Riverside into an early state of excitement. Three minutes gone, and we're one down already.

But, this is all obviously part of the plan, and Middlesbrough have fallen into the trap. Yes, we have lulled them into a false sense of security, and now we can strike. Six minutes later we do, with Manucho powering home Barmby's cross. Then he nearly puts us ahead. The plan has worked so well, we decide to try it again, and a second Boro goal is duly gifted.

However, they are getting wise to our crafty ways, and this time, it lulls them into a *true* sense of security, and we don't trouble them much before half time… or even after half time. Stuart Downing creates the best chance of the half, forcing Duke into a smart stop at his near post.

Then, with time running out, Phil Brown's best friend, Marlon King, decides to grab the salt and rub it into the proverbial wound. He robs Boateng and advances on goal for a cool finish. How we could have done with something like that at the other end.

Another winnable game has slipped through our grasp, and if we're not careful, Premiership status may slip through it too.

Character – 6 out of 10

A genuine apology to the residents of Middlesbrough here, because I know how it feels when people slag off your city without really knowing it. I'm sure there are nice parts of Middlesbrough, with charm and character; it's just that I didn't see any.

The ground is built in the middle of a godforsaken area, and although it is well designed, it has no soul. Imagine if you will, a highly advanced alien spaceship, travelling millions of light years across the universe, only to touch down in the middle of a barren lifeless plain. Such is the Riverside.

Even the stadium name is a sly 'estate agent-style' attempt to conjure up images of a more picturesque setting. Let's be honest, it should be called Dockside, and a smelly dis-used one at that.

The move from Ayresome Park took place in 1995, and they were obviously worried about leaving behind 92 years of history, so the brought a piece of it with them. The original gates from the old ground were dragged across town and positioned in front of the main entrance. It's a nice feature, but pretty useless: a bit like planting the door from your old house in the middle of your garden. Statues of Middlesbrough legends, Wilf Mannion and George Hardwick tower over the gates from either side like a couple of giant bookends. Mannion spent a season at Hull City, so they can have an extra point for that.

The atmosphere today was not great, despite the importance of the fixture, and as we lost, I'm in no mood to hand out further points unless they have been hard earned.

Summary

The journey back to Hull is one of the most depressing of the season. Joe is inconsolable, and not even the latest addition to his cuddly mascot collection can lighten the mood. Roary the Lion has been banished to the darkness of the boot, and probably won't see the light of day for quite some time.

The Easter weekend has been ruined. Even the prospect of gorging myself on mountains of chocolate tomorrow morning does not raise my spirits. But, most depressing of all, we have to do this trip all over again next weekend when we travel up to Sunderland. Will we never learn?

Matchday Experience Total – 34 out of 50

THE STADIUM OF LIGHT

Saturday 18th April 2009 – 3pm

Sunderland 1-0 Hull City

Paul Collingwood

Accessibility – 7 out of 10

A feeling of déjà vu comes over us as we stop at the McDonalds on the outskirts of York. Last week, Michele tried to superstitiously manipulate the day by carrying out a series of lucky rituals in a vain attempt to influence the result. It didn't work, but instead of dismissing all these lucky omens as a load of old tosh, she has developed a new reverse theory, whereby we have to do everything in a different way to last week. This means: sitting in different seats in the car, finding a different parking spot at McDonalds, ordering different food, and even using a different till.

But, if it's lucky omens that we're looking for, we need look no further than the sign on the A19, which reads, 'No Cats' Eyes.' Sunderland are known as the *Black Cats,* so it can only to be our advantage if they are playing blind.

We arrive early at the outskirts of Sunderland and pull into a large family pub called the *Wessington.* On the table next to us, sit a couple of Sunderland exiles, now living in Doncaster, who still travel to every Sunderland match, home and away. They don't offer much hope for their home team, but then none of the Middlesbrough fans gave their side a hope last week either.

We ask them about parking, and they suggest that our best bet will be to take advantage of the park and ride scheme just down the road. We are a little dubious about this. It may be fine for getting there, but I have disturbing visions about the fight to get on a bus afterwards, and our black and amber shirts might not be welcome if we win.

Just before we leave, Joe realises that something is caught down the inside leg of his jeans. Despite a crowded pub of onlookers, he delves deep inside to pull out the offending item. We are concerned about what might appear, but like a magician pulling a rabbit out of a hat, he produces a large white pair of Hull City shorts. It is difficult to believe that he has spent the whole day so far with these tucked inside his trousers without realising. We agree that they must be lucky pants, and insist that he wears them on top of his jeans for the rest of the day. Surprisingly, he agrees, and we leave the pub, just before he gets us thrown out.

The park and ride scheme is snubbed, and Martin heads into Sunderland, hoping for some decent parking facilities. Signs lead us to the Metro Station Car Park for the Stadium of Light, where we can stay for a fiver. A ten-minute walk over two railway bridges brings us to the ground.

Facilities – 10 out of 10

The brand spanking new aquatic centre is the first facility to catch my eye. Located right next to the stadium, it boasts an Olympic standard swimming pool and seating for over 500 spectators. Clearly, they are trying to promote the site for football and swimming with the 2012 Olympics in mind, although the Olympic committee are probably smart enough to spot that Sunderland is nearly 300 miles from London. The new building claims to be environmentally friendly by catching rainwater on the roof and filtering it for use in the pool. Should have built it in Manchester then.

Close by, stands a red and white striped hut, selling 'official club merchandise.' Predictably, no one is queuing here; they are all heading for the proper shop underneath the main stand, and so are we. Hugh buys the obligatory mug, and Joe adds to his cuddly mascot collection, although his purchase is not so straightforward. He is presented with the difficult choice of a standard male black cat, or an alternative female one with a frilly red and white striped mini skirt. He wavers for quite some time and even toys with the financial logistics of buying both, which gives me an opportunity to have a browse at the specialist jewellery and cut-glass counter. I suddenly feel as if I'm in a high street store, such is the choice of rings, watches, bracelets, champagne glasses, tankards and the like, all locked away in glass cabinets with expensive price tags. It's all very classy, except for the Sunderland logo, of course.

Joe taps me on the shoulder; he has plumped for the male cat, and we are able to move on. Hunger pangs are suppressed until we are inside the ground, and this turns out to be a wise decision. The wide selection of food and drink gazumps anything that I've seen so far this season.

Pasties, sausage rolls, hot dogs, burgers and pizzas: it's hard to choose, but I select the pizza pod, on the basis that it sounds interesting. It's not. I'm served up with a small folded pizza in a cardboard holder, but it tastes okay. For liquid refreshment, a number of people have been tempted by the two-pint measure of lager, although it doesn't come in a delicate cut-glass container. Also on the menu, we have wines and spirits, which are rarely on offer inside a stadium. This place must be absolute heaven for obese alcoholics.

The Stadium – 9 out of 10

The main entrance of the stadium possesses a smart brick-built frontage, and I'm suddenly overcome by a compulsion to dart across the car park in search of a photographic vantage point. By teetering on the banks of the River Wear, it is just about possible to squeeze it all into my viewfinder.

Attempts at close range snaps, though, are obstructed by a strange little statue that fills the foreground. It depicts a happy family, linking hands, facing outwards, holding the world aloft. Nobody seems to understand what it is in aid of.

It's a hive of activity in this area, with hundreds of fans buzzing around, awaiting the team coach. The media are here too, and we soon attract the attention of a reporter from the City Magazine. It must be Martin's furry tiger headgear that draws him in, or maybe Joe's lucky outer pants. Martin and I are asked to do a piece on camera, but Joe fails the 'fit and proper person's test.'

Pleased with our slick and accomplished interviews, we move along, until we bump into another commemorative statue. This one shows Bob Stokoe running across the Wembley pitch in 1973, and it bears the legend: 'The Man, The Messiah, The Moment.' Just behind it, Kevin Day is conducting an interview for *Match of the Day 2,* but we fail to muscle in on this one.

On the other side of the turnstiles, the Stadium of Light continues to impress. After popping my Pizza Pod, I negotiate a ramp, which leads to the seating area, and as expected, the seats are all red. Then I look more closely at the lower tier, which has suffered from prolonged exposure to the sun, and I realise that they have all turned a fetching shade of pink.

Half of the stadium is two-tiered, but a third tier runs along the top of the West and North Stands. Several international flags are draped over the edge of this, apparently representing Sunderland fan clubs from around the world. (Yeah, in their dreams). The capacity is a striking 48,000; double that of the KC.

The Match – 5 out of 10

The first half is quite open, with chances at both ends. We come closest with a Kilbane header, which forces Craig Gordon into a low diving parry, but just when we appear to be revving up for a second half onslaught, Sunderland score. We've suffered our fair share of dopey linesmen this season, and today is no exception, so Cisse's offside position is totally ignored as he nods Sunderland into the lead.

They say that you get no luck when you're struggling at the wrong end of the league, but luck certainly doesn't appear to be deserting jammy Sunderland. Cisse goes embarrassingly bonkers when he scores, and he runs into the arms of his adoring fans, but he has just ripped the shirt off his sweaty body in celebration, so cuddles are not too forthcoming. The French tattooed hair-obsessed poser gets a booking for this, which will incense his manager. It never ceases to amaze me how players will still strip to the waist, despite the certainty of receiving a yellow card. Mind you, it's been a while for Cisse.

I assume that he would exercise greater restraint, were he to score a second, and we very nearly get to find out early in the second half when his goal-bound strike is beaten out by Myhill. Boeteng responds with a flashing volley, which whistles inches wide. A header from Kenwyne Jones is then ruled out for offside, suggesting that they have used up all their luck.

Folan comes close with a header, but Sunderland hang on for the vital win, allowing them to leapfrog us in the Premiership table.

Character – 6 out of 10

The statue of Bob Stokoe captures an important piece of Sunderland's history, although it seems a little out of place here, at the new stadium. Stokoe's success was achieved at Roker Park, which they left in 1997.

Paul Collingwood

The move also saw a change in the official club nickname, with fans voting for the Black Cats. Previously, they had been better known as the Mackems, Rokerites or Roker Men. The new name links back to the Black Cat Battery Gun, which was stationed nearby on the River Wear. I suppose they couldn't really call themselves the Gunners.

Sunderland is a side with a proud history of honours, including six league title wins. It's just a shame that most fans are not old enough to remember them, the last one being in 1936.

Summary

It's another thoroughly miserable journey home. For the first time this season, I begin to believe that we may actually go down. We're just finding it so hard to score goals. Only once since Christmas have we managed to score twice in a Premiership match, and that was against the bottom club. It doesn't bode well.

Matchday Experience Total – 37 out of 50

VILLA PARK

Monday 4th May 2009 – 8pm

Aston Villa 1-0 Hull City

Accessibility – 7 out of 10

Yet again, Sky TV fiddle about with the fixture schedule, totally wrecking everyone's plans for the bank holiday weekend. A late Monday night kick off means that we'll all struggle to get in for work on the Tuesday morning; never an enjoyable experience, and even more unbearable when we lose.

I set off extra early, guessing that the roads might be clogged on this May Day holiday, but they are not, so I treat myself to a break at Corley services, where I relax with a cappuccino and a newspaper, surrounded by Villa fans.

The City website recommends coming off the M6 at Junction 7 from the north. I decide to run with these directions, even though I'm coming up from the south. This brings me along the A34 until I arrive at a greyhound track. Apparently, I will find lots of sign posts here for £4 car parks, but they must be bloody well hidden. After a bit of aimless driving around, I eventually come across a clutch of £5 car parks. I feel cheated.

A steward relieves me of a fiver, before assuring me, with great precision, that it is a seven-minute walk to the ground. He's got it just about right.

Facilities – 6 out of 10

Close to the ground, I pass the Aston Hotel, which looks like an ideal spot for a pre-match drink, until I spy the stroppy sign: 'Strictly no away fans!' I carry on to the ground. I know when I'm not welcome.

The McAllisters are waiting by the Doug Ellis Stand, next to the away turnstiles, but we are not ready to enter yet. Our first port of call is the Holte End, where we loiter for a while in the car park. There are plenty of burger wagons here, and a large screen is rotating on a thick metal post, very much like the sign outside Scotland Yard.

As I view the latest team news, a couple of trainee hooligans, aged about eight, begin to taunt me. 'Your gonna lose,' they keep chanting in broad brummie. 'You're rubbish.'

I'm about to retaliate, but then I realise that they are probably right, and I congratulate them on their insight. This confuses them, and they run off to pick on someone their own size.

Back at the turnstiles, the penultimate addition to Hugh's mug collection nearly gets us turned away. The steward can't understand why a Hull City fan would be concealing an Aston Villa mug inside his jacket, and he becomes very suspicious. Hugh is forced to explain about his obsessive hobby, and we are reluctantly allowed to pass.

An awful lot of stairs need to be negotiated before we finally arrive at the upper tier. We push through some double doors, and find ourselves in an extremely narrow corridor. A small hatch is serving a limited range of refreshments, and the customers are forced to queue sideways in a very long line, with their backs pressed against the wall. Normally, in this situation, we would assess the length of other queues further down, but there is little point; this is the only outlet. We don't even consider joining the line. The facilities are unbelievably inadequate for such a large stand. Maybe this is why the away fans were switched to this section a couple of seasons ago.

The Stadium – 9 out of 10

Our walk to the Holte End Car Park is worth it for the view of the brick façade and multitude of steps leading up to it. At the base, sits the posh-looking Holte Suite, but this is members only, and a couple of hefty bouncers are stationed in the entrance to make sure that it stays this way. From afar, the whole stand looks like some kind of huge fortress.

Inside, the view from the upper tier of the Doug Ellis Stand makes up for the disappointment of the poxy little food hatch. The three-tiered Trinity Road Stand sits opposite, and this is as good as any stand I've seen this season. The Holte End is far away to my left, and the North Stand is just to my right.

Fortunately, the McAllisters are not sitting with me. I say this, because my ticket places me in seat no. 13, and Michele is hugely superstitious. She would be unable to cope with the curse that this bestows upon the Tigers. I'm more concerned with the position of the seat, which is out on a limb, in the corner of the ground. The view o the game would be excellent, if only it were taking place in the North Stand car park, just below me, to the right.

I'm on the front row, and a brave young lad next to me clearly feels that this is a safe enough position to direct a number of rude hand gestures to the lower tier of the North Stand.

The choral banter between fans is healthy and humorous, but my hostile neighbour is determined to make eye contact with anyone that he can, as he offers them the middle finger and a succession of masturbation mimes, which he seems particularly good at: must have had lots of practice.

The Match – 6 out of 10

I know I've said this a number of times since Christmas, but we look good in the opening ten minutes. Ashbee then gets injured, and is forced to leave the action. Marney gets a run as his replacement, and Villa get on top.

After a couple of wayward Villa efforts, our fans let rip with a couple of verses of:

'Champions League, you're having a laugh…'

I sing along, but I just know that we are setting ourselves up here, and it doesn't take long for the Villains to come back with a couple of predictable responses:

'Premiership, you're having a laugh,' and 'You're going down with the Baggies.'

Just when we are looking comfortable, Villa strike. Boeteng gets robbed in their half, allowing them to break at pace. Ashley Young floats in a tempting cross, and Carew steals in unmarked, but surely offside, to put them ahead. The giant centre forward has a long hopeful look at the linesman before daring to celebrate. My brother, Mike, texts me from Spain to confirm that it was at least three millimetres offside. Typical. We never get the benefit of the doubt in these situations.

We don't look too threatening at the other end until Geovanni bursts through and drags a shot wide. Cousin clearly feels that the Brazilian should have put it on a plate for him, and an argument ensues. This continues as they head to the tunnel for the half time break, and Geovanni does not return for the second half. Barmby is his replacement.

This does not fill me with optimism, and it crosses my mind that if I set off for home now, I can return at a reasonable hour, instead of midnight.

Villa continue to dominate, but Myhill is determined to keep us in it with some great saves against his former employers. One of these is made with his face, at point-blank range from a Carew header. This time, he really is offside, by a mile, and I don't need the benefit of a replay, because I'm right in line with it. Scandalously, the linesman keeps his flag down. I can only think that he must be a Newcastle fan.

In the final ten minutes, the Tigers go looking for an equaliser, and we very nearly get it. We actually pin Villa back into their own half for considerable spells, but it just won't drop for us. Time runs out, and another opportunity to pull away from the drop zone goes begging.

Character – 9 out of 10

The club and the stadium are steeped in history. Villa Park has been Aston Villa's home since 1897, and much has been achieved in that time. There has been much talk this season of Villa breaking into the top four, but ironically, if you add up all the honours that they have won since formation, they are the fourth most successful side in England. The trouble is, they've won nothing since 1996, and that was only the League Cup.

It is a great stadium to visit. It looks good on the outside and the inside, and the design of the Holte End gives it bonus points. When City got promoted to the Premiership, this was one of the grounds that I most wanted to visit, and it hasn't let me down. Shame that City did.

Paul Collingwood

Summary

Earlier in the weekend, all of our main rivals had lost, prompting the press to describe this game as a 'free hit.' I wasn't too keen on this term, as it implied that it didn't really matter if we lost. I preferred to think of it as a golden opportunity – to open up a gap on our rivals. Either way, we blew it, and it could be costly.

Matchday Experience Total – 37 out of 50

THE REEBOK STADIUM

Saturday 16th May 2009 – 3pm

Bolton Wanderers 1-1 Hull City

Accessibility – 8 out of 10

Seven of us travel in convoy from Hull to Bolton, in three cars, so we're not really doing our bit for the environment. This is because I need to travel straight back to Hemel Hempstead after the game. Cousin Stephen jumps in with me and spends the journey selecting feel good songs from my CD collection.

Each tune seems to bear special significance to the must-win encounter with Bolton. A couple of tracks from the Stereophonics go down well. Hopefully we *will* 'Have a Nice Day.' My favourite, though, must be Feeder's *Buck Rodgers*, which includes the relevant lyric, 'this time we're gonna make it!'

The music puts us in a positive frame of mind as we bounce across the Pennines, and we soon convince ourselves that the Tigers will triumph, despite having lost the last five.

I don't really pay much attention to where we're going. I just blindly follow Hugh and Michele along the M62, M60 and M61. Fortunately, the Reebok is well sign-posted and it is close to the motorway. We are soon peeling off into the Bolton suburb of Horwich in search of a watering hole.

Facilities – 9 out of 10

Martin has taken advice from the Fanzine website, which highly recommends the Bromilow Arms. This well-established pub is a fifteen-minute walk from the ground, but you can leave your car in their car park, without charge. What a result!

The weather-beaten exterior is in dire need of a makeover, but the same cannot be said of the inside, due to a unique method of decoration. Every square inch of the ceiling and walls has been covered by an extensive collection of football shirts and scarves, past and present.

The first ones to catch my eye, stapled to a crossbeam, are from Dundee United and Shrewsbury. The next five minutes are spent rotating our tilted heads in search of something from Hull City, but we have been overlooked. Hugh promises that we'll return with one next season, but the barman has already taken a fancy to Joe's signed

Geovanni top. The deal is, that the signed tops get framed behind the bar, but with no money appearing to be on the negotiating table, it's 'No Deal.'

In the corner, by the television, hangs a Carl Zeiss Jena scarf. This generates an enlightening discussion. We have just established that it was an East German side, when Hugh thrusts his camcorder under our noses. Inscribed on the lens rim are the words 'Carl Zeiss.' Apparently, the club was formed by Carl's optics company in the German city of Jena, back in the early 1900's. Well, you learn something new every day.

Across at the pool table, Michael and Stephen decide to take on Martin and Joe, but I'm paying more attention to the European section of the ceiling above their heads. Initially, I thought that generous visiting fans must have donated all the memorabilia, but the Ajax and Juventus tops make me suspicious: maybe in pre-season friendlies?

On balance, it would be well worth sacrificing my £40 replica Tigers shirt, but only if it is guaranteed a prominent central position. It is certainly a fascinating pub, and I could sit and gawp at the ceiling all day, but we eventually move on to the ground, before we all get stiff necks.

The first port of call at the stadium is the club shop. This is large and well stocked, and a manikin stands at the centre, proudly sporting the new Bolton kit for next season. The logo for 188BET is in the middle of the shirt, with a random collection of black vertical stripes below, looking a lot like a large barcode.

The designers of the ground have cleverly placed a cash machine right outside the shop. A sign above reads, 'Goal in the Wall.' Michele works in a bank and she finds the little pun hilarious. We are delayed while she takes several photos. Her colleagues are in for a real treat on Monday morning.

A better photo opportunity is presented just around the corner. The empty Hull City team coach is parked by the side of the road, and Martin somehow persuades the driver to let Michele take the wheel. This is very kind of the man, or possibly irresponsible, and he definitely begins to look a bit edgy as we all pile on board, and he ponders how he might explain this one to the police should Michele thrust it into gear and take us for a tour.

Inside the ground, I join Michael and Stephen in the queue for grub. The queues are of the lengthy variety, probably because we have brought 5,200 fans. I can remember the days when we would have been thrilled to get that at Boothferry Park. The tedious shuffle towards the bar is made bearable by the TV screens, which are showing Man Utd's clash with Arsenal. Unusually, all 5,200 City fans are cheering for United. A win or a draw will hand them the title, allowing the reserves to get a run at the KC next week, while the big guns are saved for the Champions League Final.

The food options turn out to be very good. I go for the Cheeseburger, and Stephen risks the Chicken Balti Pie. Alcohol comes in the form of lager or white wine. We choose lager. A Mars Bar assumes the role of pudding.

The Old Trafford match ends in a 0-0 draw, pleasing the whole of the South Stand. A chorus of, 'We are staying up,' breaks out. It's a shame that we are starting to rely so heavily on other teams to do us a favour. Suddenly, the concourse empties, and everyone shuffles out into the sunshine to inspect the ground.

Stadium – 9 out of 10

This is one of the better Premiership grounds, sitting in a scenic location, surrounded by gently rolling hills. It benefits from some unique architecture too. A network of thick white tubular girders converges at the four corners before rising up to support the floodlights. These lean in towards the pitch, giving the impression that some serious subsidence is going on, but I'm sure it's all a deliberate part of the design. From afar, it has the look of a giant rectangular birthday cake that has sunk in the middle due to a carelessly opened oven door.

On the inside, two-tiered stands rise up to a good height on all sides. The lower tiers join up at the corners; the curved upper tiers don't. I'm in the lower tier of the South Stand, behind the goal.

The capacity is 28,000 and with a packed City end, it shouldn't be far off that today. As kick off approaches, there are still plenty of gaps in the home end, prompting the City fans to sing: 'Your ground's too big for you!'

The Match – 7 out of 10

It may be a vital game, but City settle well, and carve out the better chances. Trouble is, we don't take any, and Jaaskelainen, once again, looks set to play the role of party-pooper. Sure enough, after 25 minutes we are punished for our wastefulness when Steinsson's speculative low shot squirms through Myhill's defences. I really should be getting used to that awful sinking feeling that invades the stomach pit when City concede, but this one really hurts, and I can feel the icy fingers of relegation resting on my shoulders.

City come again, but Manucho blazes miles over after a brilliant run by Ricketts. The ref gives a corner, unable to believe that a professional footballer could possibly clear the bar by such a huge margin without some kind of defensive intervention.

On the stroke of half time, Craig Fagan makes a crucial goal line clearance to keep us in it. Such standard actions suddenly take on huge significance at this stage of the season. Every save, block, miss or goal is viewed potentially as the one that keeps us up or takes us down. I slope off for a half time coffee, a mightily relieved man.

Michael and Stephen are seated on the opposite side of the stand, so I have to barge my way through a mass of bodies before I can meet up for the first half post-mortem. We unanimously agree that City deserve better, but it's been the story of our season (well, since December 13th, anyway).

Our in-depth analysis becomes a bit too involved; giving the two teams no choice but to start the second half without us. We are oblivious to the resumption, until an almighty roar comes rolling down into the concourse from out in the stand. Everyone suddenly tries to crush through the small stairwell to see what has happened. The noise seemed too close for it to be a Bolton goal, and sure enough, the whole of the South Stand is dancing with delight, singing: 'We are staying up!'

A quick glance at the big screen confirms the change in the scoreline, but it doesn't confirm the scorer. I ask around, but most people near me appear to have missed it too. Someone thinks it was Fagan. The non-stop action continues on the pitch, and I'm reluctant to move from my new position (standing in the aisle, blocking everyone's view).

Eventually, a burly steward convinces me that it would be in my best interests to budge, so I do. No more key action is missed while I make the short journey back to my original seat. Here, my neighbour informs me that Shittu was to blame for Fagan's goal, dithering in defence to allow the City striker sight of the target. I seem to remember the big defender being equally compliant in last year's play offs against Watford. He has had quite an influence on City's most successful period, without ever playing for us.

From this point on, City take complete control, and a string of chances are created: Barmby hits the post; Cousin hits the bar, and Marney fires across goal, but all to no avail. Finally, a perfect cross from Halmosi appears to have set up a glorious winner, but Fagan's diving header is palmed away by Jussi 'Bastard' Jaaskelainen.

It ends in a draw, and I wonder just when our luck will start to turn. But, maybe it already has. News filters through that Newcastle have lost at home to Fulham, and they had a perfectly good goal disallowed. It drags us out of the bottom three. This point could yet prove to be very precious.

Character – 6 out of 10

Bolton were one of the twelve founding members of the Football League back in 1888, so they have a massive tradition, although they've never won the title. In fact, they hold the unenviable record of completing the highest number of seasons in the top division without ever winning the thing. This year is their 70th attempt. The Tigers, of course, hold the record for the fewest attempts – just the one so far!

Occupancy at the Reebok was taken up in 1997, after a 102 year stay at Burnden Park, so there is little evidence of their proud history, apart from the Nat Lofthouse Stand, named after their most celebrated player. He scored in the 1958 FA Cup triumph and played in the famous Matthews Cup final of 1953, where Bolton acted as the fall guys to Blackpool.

Summary

Craig Fagan certainly made a telling contribution today: a goal line clearance, a vital goal, and very nearly a winner.

But now, it all hinges on our final home game against the English, European and World Champions. What was it we all said with a chuckle last June when the fixtures came out?

'Let's hope we're not needing points from that one to stay up!'

Will we be chuckling at tea-time next Sunday?

Matchday Experience Total – 39 out of 40

Survival Sunday – 24th May 2009

Tickets for the end of season clash with Manchester United were always going to be difficult to come by. Instead, I find myself at a 21st birthday party, in a back garden in Twickenham, sandwiched between an Ipswich fan and a Fulham fan.

The Premiership fixtures have not yet kicked off, but Leo is already welcoming me back to the Championship, and is making arrangements for my visit to Portman Road.

Steve is also having a good gloat. He still hasn't forgiven me for Manucho's late Craven Cottage winner back in March, taking the defeat as a personal insult, after he was kind enough to wangle me a discount ticket in the Neutral Stand. Steve's surname is Rothwell, so Manucho's memorable strike is now remembered within our circle as the 'Rothwell Incident.'

Malcolm sat beside me on that famous night, but today he is manning the barbecue with a radio by his side, ready to keep us abreast of all the developments across the grounds.

The television is on inside, showing all the relevant action, but only my son, Stephen (a Manchester United fan) can bear to watch. My preferred strategy is to down as many pints of Stella as possible, acting as an anaesthetic against any painful twists and turns that may lie ahead.

This is supposed to be a Hawaiian Cocktail Party, and most guests have complied with the tropical dress code of loud shirts, hula skirts and exotic flowers in the hair. I'm not a fan of fancy dress parties at the best of times, and I've stubbornly refused to join in, just in case the afternoon turns into the 'worst of times.'

Similarly, for the Play Off Final last year, I resisted the temptation to paint my face and wear a funny wig. Somehow, pre-match optimism and beer creates complete immunity from self-consciousness with many giddy fans before a big match, and they will happily wear the most embarrassing costumes. But beware; it's guaranteed that in defeat, the television cameras will pick you out, and you will look like a sad prat.

At precisely twenty past four, Stephen comes rushing out of the house, yelling, 'One nil – Gibson – what a goal – come on Man U.'

I feel betrayed. My very own son, twisting the knife as our Premiership dream slips away, after only one bite at the cherry. Leo starts to give me directions from the M25 to Ipswich. I reach for another lager.

Ten minutes later, loud cheering can be heard from the KC, via Malcolm's radio. City haven't scored though; Villa have, against Newcastle, putting the Toon back into the bottom three. This could be going on all afternoon. I sink some more beer, which curiously, tastes a lot better now.

Time continues to tick away, very slowly, but no more news is forthcoming. No news is good news, but I am painfully aware that a Newcastle goal will change everything.

As the second halves progress, I edge nearer to the radio, and then I sneak inside to endure the final minutes visually. I just want it all to be over, so that the pain will go away. I want my appetite to return, so I can eat some of Malcolm's burnt offerings. The lager strategy is having little effect.

The final whistle goes at the KC, and the action switches to Villa Park for Newcastle's final desperate attempts at survival. Villa appear to be on the attack, which is reassuring. Then, I'm suddenly watching shots of a glum Alan Shearer (Hull City's Messiah) shaking hands with Martin O'Niell. It's all over. We're safe!

I let out an involuntary scream, and guests come running through in a panic to see who has been murdered. They soon realise what all the fuss is about, and for a little while I become the main attraction, receiving a number of congratulatory handshakes and heartfelt hugs from football fans who understand what this means to me.

In the doorway, 21-year-old Chris is looking a little put out. This was supposed to be his party.

Final Score

It was a tight contest in the end. Every matchday experience was enjoyable, and only 12 points separated first place from last. I must admit, it pains me to place Manchester United at the top, but they probably only made it because of the museum and the seven-goal thriller. If I was to go on the stadium and facilities alone, I think Arsenal and Manchester City would be the winners.

Here are the final places:

Stadium	Points
1. Old Trafford	42
2. The Emirates Stadium	41
3. Anfield	40
4. The Reebok Stadium	39
City of Manchester Stadium	39
5. Craven Cottage	38
6. Villa Park	37
The Stadium of Light	37
7. St. James' Park	36
8. Stamford Bridge	35
The Hawthorns	35
9. The KC Stadium	34
Whitehart Lane	34
The Riverside Stadium	34

Acknowledgments

With thanks to:

Patsy Collingwood, for letting me off the leash twenty times.

Elizabeth, Emma and Stephen Collingwood, for allowing me to monopolise the computer for the last year.

Dave Coward, for supplying me with most of the match tickets.

Michele, Hugh, Martin and Joe McAllister, for lifting me to Newcastle, Middlesbrough and Sunderland. Also, for their company at most games.

The rest of the cast, in order of appearance:

Mike Collingwood
Peter Collingwood
Peter Tisi & Joe Tisi
Michael & Stephen McGeown
Gary Hogben
Ben Cawthorn
Chris Clark
Chris Coward
Vin Kerr
Ian Appleyard
Steve & Peter Dyas
Bob Bayley

Graham – the Nutter on the Tube
Mike Suffield
Colin Crowe
Brian Clancy
Maura & Kevin Clancy
Malcolm Hill
Steve Rothwell
Jeremy Lonsdale
Dave Ledger
Leo Brennan
Chris Hill